The Entrepreneur's Guide Series

MASTERING THE BUSINESS CYCLE

How to Keep Your Company on Track In Times of Economic Change

Albert N. Link

PROBUS PUBLISHING COMPANY
Chicago, Illinois

Library of Congress Cataloging-in-Publication Data

Mastering the business cycle : how to keep your company on track in
   times of economic change / Albert N. Link, editor.
       p.   cm. -- (The Entrepreneur's guide series)
   Includes index.
   ISBN 1-55738-144-5 : $19.95
   1. Crisis management. 2. Business cycles--Management. I. Link,
Albert N. II. Series.
HD49.M37   1991
658.4--dc20
                                                    90-20876
                                                       CIP

Printed in the United States of America
BC
1 2 3 4 5 6 7 8 9 0

Additional Titles in
The Entrepreneur's Guide Series
Available from Probus Publishing

Table of Contents

Preface

Over the years, entrepreneurs have worn many masks and have played many roles: risk takers, financiers, innovators, decision makers, corporate leaders, managers, organizers, owners, contractors, and arbitrageurs. As a result, entrepreneurs have made it their business to be better informed about economic events. Thus, they have held a comparative advantage over their counterparts in that they have been able to make decisions when others were unsure and to take advantage of events when others hesitated.

This, of course, is what this book is all about. Swings in business cycles are natural events; but they are two-edged. They afford opportunities to those with the skills and understanding to take advantage of them. But they also can hurt, even destroy, the growing business.

This book is directed toward owners, managers, and advisors of growing businesses who wish to take a more sophisticated approach to business planning and decision making. First, you will learn what business cycles are and what makes them happen. Then, you will learn how to use economic indicators to help with your business planning. Finally, you will see, through everyday business examples, the importance of understanding and anticipating business cycles. Throughout the book I will set forth prescriptions based on my experience as a consultant and on my training as an economist. These are suggestions and I urge you to take them in that light. Changes in business practices should not be made as a result of reading this or any other single book. Rather, my purpose, and the purpose of many other authors, is to challenge you to think about your management practices in new ways and set a direction as to how you may begin to initiate change.

No book is an individual effort. I want to thank the people at Probus for their continued support throughout this project. I also want to thank James Ogburn, Sabrina Woodbery, and Peter Saffo for their constructive comments. And, there is my wonderful, patient family, without whose support and kind words this project would never have been completed. This book is dedicated to them.

Albert N. Link

CHAPTER 1
An Introduction to Business Cycles

I was a-trembling because I'd got to decide forever betwixt two things, and I knowed it. I studied for a minute, sort of holding my breath, and then says to myself, "All right, then, I'll go to hell."

Adventures of Huckleberry Finn

Business cycles are natural events. Over the business cycle key economic variables change. These variables include interest rates, inflation, employment levels, incomes, and profit. Anticipating these changes can greatly enhance your profit, whereas unanticipated changes can have a detrimental impact on your business. You should be aware that there is information available to help you anticipate business cycles.

Consider Huckleberry Finn's predicament. If he only had known what the future had in store his choice might have been different! The same was true for Bill Lawrence, vice president of production at a midwestern manufacturer of electronic components. Based on informal feedback from their marketing and sales people, there was an expectation that demand would remain strong or even grow for at least another year to year-and-a-half. Using this information, Bill obligated his company to purchase

1

over $600,000 of new component parts. Two months later the economy slowed and consumers' demand fell off sharply. Bill's company had the largest third quarter loss of the past ten years. If only Bill had known what the economy was going to do.

Unfortunately, there is no insurance against a bad decision. I wish there were. Had Bill been better informed, his misjudgment might not have occurred. How was he to have known that the economy would turn down? Can such events be anticipated? What should he have done differently?

Information is invaluable when making business decisions. The better informed you are, the more likely you will make a good decision.

For any business, a critical question is: what economic conditions will prevail in the future? While some argue that forecasting is nothing more than a fanciful exercise, it is my belief that forecasting, even on a limited scale, can yield bountiful harvests.

Every business operates in an economic environment characterized by cyclical change. These cycles are not random events. They can be anticipated to some degree, and information about them can be of enormous help to the conscientious manager.

Business cycles create favorable and unfavorable business climates. For example, as we saw with Bill Lawrence, it was not a profitable move to expand production in the face of a developing recession. The same would have been true if Bill had tried to introduce a new product. On the other hand, it can be very profitable for a business to introduce a new product when the economy is poised for an upturn.

There are many other examples of the importance of timing when making business decisions. Most corporations acquire long term debt. It is generally in their best interest to do so when interest rates are low (i.e., when the economy is slowing down) rather than when interest rates are high. Similarly, inventories are preferred when demand is high, but not when it is low.

We live in a cyclical economy; that fact will not change. Managers must therefore have a clear understanding of business cycles, the economic forces that cause then, and the business implications of changes in the economy.

WHAT IS A BUSINESS CYCLE?

A business cycle consists of alternating periods of expansion and contraction of economic activity.

Over time, there is a natural tendency for any economy to experience fluctuations in activity. In addition to this natural tendency, macroeconomic policies (e.g., changes in tax rates or changes in the money supply) influence the direction of the economy. It is difficult, if not impossible, to separate natural swings in the economy from those due to policy (well-formulated or otherwise). For the most part, that distinction is not critical for a manager. What is important is the ability to anticipate business cycles (i.e., perception) and to plan around them (i.e., action). Such abilities—perception and action—characterize entrepreneurs.

A business cycle is illustrated in Figure 1.1. This cycle, like all cycles, has two defining characteristics—a peak and a trough. Several phases are in between as explained in Table 1.1.

Figure 1.1
A Business Cycle

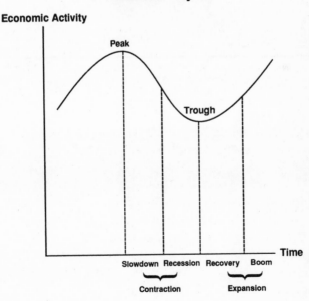

Table 1.1
Phases of a Business Cycle

Phase of the Cycle	Characteristics
Contraction Phase	Economic activity declining
Slowdown	Initial period of decline following a peak
Recession	Prolonged period of decline leading to a trough
Expansion Phase	Economic activity increasing
Recovery	Initial period of recovery following a trough
Boom	Prolonged period of recovery leading to a peak

Expansions and contractions are associated with cyclical movements in key economic variables. In an expansion, interest rates, the rate of inflation, the level of employment, and real (meaning adjusted for inflation) income and after tax profit generally increase. These variables move in the opposite direction during a contraction. It is not surprising that each is often referred to as being cyclical in nature. These cyclical trends are summarized in Table 1.2 for later reference.

Most managers agree that they would like to anticipate economic changes more accurately. The problem is that no one knows where the economy actually is until after it has gotten there. We

Table 1.2
Behavior of Key Economic Variables
over the Business Cycle

Economic Variable	Phase of the Business Cycle	
	Expansion	Contraction
Interest Rates	Increase	Decrease
Rate of Inflation	Increases	Decreases
Level of Employment	Increases	Decreases
Level of Unemployment	Decreases	Increases
Real Income	Increases	Decreases
Real After Tax Profit	Increases	Decreases

have to look back on economic activity and determine, after the fact, that a peak or a trough was reached.

The consequences of a misperception were illustrated clearly in the Bill Lawrence example. He thought the economy was experiencing an extended period of expansion. That is, Bill thought the economy was at point A in Figure 1.2. He expected the expansion to last another twelve to eighteen months (point B) and he made the necessary decisions. He was wrong and he realized this after the fact. His actions are evaluated in Table 1.3.

Bill's predicament is not unusual. You only need to glance through business magazines to see many examples where poor timing or unanticipated economic events had a detrimental effect on a business's profitability. Donald Trump's multi-million dollar casino opened in Atlantic City when our economy was in the midst of a prolonged economic slowdown and did not start off with the bang that was anticipated at its conception.

Figure 1.2
What Will Economic Activity Do in the Future?

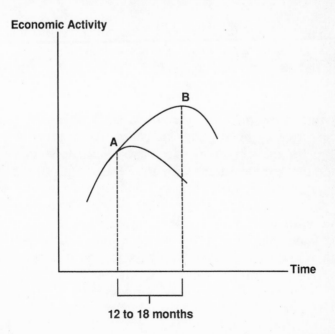

Table 1.3
Evaluation of Bill Lawrence's Actions

As It Happened	*Critique*
Bill expected the demand for the company's products to remain strong for at least 12 to 18 months.	His expectation was based on informal feedback from marketing and sales people. He did not take into account any forecasts about the economy as a whole.
Bill purchased a large number of component parts based on his expectation of continued strong demand.	Had Bill thought that there was a chance that the economy would slow down, he might have contracted for periodic purchases rather than making one bulk purchase.

HOW CAN A BUSINESS CYCLE INFLUENCE YOUR BUSINESS?

A good manager takes many things into account before making a decision. Critical among these are anticipated changes in the key economic variables listed in Table 1.2.

Interest Rates

An interest rate is the price of borrowing money. As interest rates increase, the price of borrowing increases. As interest rates decrease, the price of borrowing decreases. Higher interest rates mean higher interest payments. An important component of the cost of, for example, building a new building or purchasing new equipment is the interest payment on the loan. Because these payments move with the level of interest rates, the cost of physical growth varies over the business cycle. In response, the demand for construction activity varies over the cycle, as does the profitability of the construction companies and equipment suppliers.

Interest rates also affect the cost of acquiring debt. Corporations acquire operating funds in a number of ways. Two common ways are to issue equity (stocks) and to issue debt (bonds). Issuing debt is the same as borrowing money from investors. They receive an IOU, called a bond, and you receive money which you are obligated to repay with interest. Therefore, the cost of acquiring debt also varies over the cycle.

The housing industry is very sensitive to movements in interest rates because those rates directly affect individuals' mortgage payments and thus their ability to qualify for home loans. When interest rates rise (fall), the mortgage portion of the cost of purchasing a home increases (decreases). Swings in interest rates affect the profitability of the entire housing industry, especially those businesses that produce products used in home construction or for home furnishings.

Inflation

Inflation refers to a period of rising prices. Deflation refers to a period of falling prices, but we have not seen one in many years. Generally, prices increase at a faster rate during an expansion than during a contraction. This is true for all prices, not just the price of final goods and services. It is true for the price of factors of production. Such factors include raw materials and labor. Customers (referring to final consumers as well as companies that purchase inputs from other companies) decrease their quantity demanded as prices increase. This is fundamental to the so-called Law of Demand.

Employment

Changes in employment levels can also affect a business. When unemployment levels are low toward the end of an expansion, it is difficult to find capable employees. This is troubling because demand is strong. Because demand is strong and profit is high, competitors are in a good position to pay top dollar for new employees. They frequently will try to hire key personnel away from competitors. To keep such personnel, higher in-house salaries must be offered. But these higher salaries are then passed along to consumers in the form of higher product prices. Higher prices then dampen customers' demand. We have a circular chain of events which can lead eventually to an economic slowdown.

Real Income and After Tax Profit

As real income and real after tax profit increase, customers are in a favorable position to purchase more goods and services. Sales and profit increase as does the need for greater production capacity. But, the rising interest rates associated with this growth will increase the cost of financing the needed capacity.

You probably already detect what seem to be some contradictory trends. You might be saying to yourself, "I thought that businesses expand when the economy is growing." That is true. Generally, the influence of increasing sales and profit on expansion often outweighs the increased cost associated with higher interest rates, but not always. Managers have to take all of these elements into account when making decisions. I note these piecemeal effects only to introduce you to the idea that there are countervailing forces present during a business cycle and unanticipated changes in these forces will affect your business and its profitability. In the real world they occur simultaneously.

THE MANAGER'S VIEWPOINT

I asked 70 presidents/CEOs from U.S. companies how closely they watch business cycle movements. As you can see from the responses in Table 1.4, 55 of the 70 top executives pay at least moderate attention to business cycle movements. Those paying the least attention are in the service sector or are new, high-tech companies heavily involved with new product development. To me, it appears that corporate America watches and anticipates cycles closely.

See Appendix A.1 for details about how these responses were obtained.

Table 1.4
How Closely Managers Watch the Business Cycle

How closely do you watch the business cycle?

Type of Company	Very Closely	Moderately Closely	Not Very Closely	Not at All
Manufacturing (40)	31	8	1	0
Service (15)	9	4	2	0
High Tech (15)	1	8	5	1

ACTION ITEMS

☞ Because changes in key economic variables over the business cycle significantly influence your business, make efforts to learn more about the business cycle. Have your key subordinates do the same.

☞ Keep in mind that all business cycle information is based on composite forecasts of what is expected to be in store for the economy. As such, remember that this information may be subject to error.

☞ Your competitors are using as much information about the future state of the economy as possible in making their business plans. You should be equally well informed.

SECTION 1
The Nature of Business Cycles

CHAPTER 2
Recent Business Cycles

Uneven economic and political development is an absolute law of capitalism.

Nikolai Lenin

Business cycles are an economic fact of life, but they do not occur with predictable regularity. Business cycles exist in every economy; however, all business cycles are not alike. Most industrialized countries experience similar, but not identical, business cycles.

It would be accurate to elaborate upon Lenin's thought by saying that business cycles are not just an "economic law of capitalism" but also they are an economic fact of life. All economies have their ups and downs. For the most part, these economic swings result from similar market forces. The primary culprit is changes in aggregate (meaning economywide) demand. Uneven changes in demand bring about uneven changes in economic activity. We thus have business cycles.

ARE ALL BUSINESS CYCLES ALIKE?

The two diagrams in Figure 2.1 show the cyclical nature of the U.S. economy over the past 120 years. Before commenting on specific patterns, it is important to point out that economic activity in the upper diagram is measured by the growth rate in real gross national product (GNP). Briefly, GNP refers to the dollar value of all goods and services sold in the economy in a given year. Economic activity is measured by the rate of inflation in the lower diagram.

Real GNP and the inflation rate are two of several measures of economic activity. Both show similar patterns of activity. The reason for this similarity is that changes in real GNP reflect changes in aggregate demand, and inflation is nothing more than the price response to changing demand. Other measures of economic activity are described in Exhibit 2.1.

You can see from either of the diagrams that all business cycles are not alike. Exhibit 2.2 elaborates on the fact that cycles differ over time. Some cycles last longer than others, and some exhibit more dramatic swings than others. Compare in Figure 2.1 the magnitude of the swings after World War I and during World War II to the activity in the post-Korean War period. Also compare in Figure 2.1 the length of the nearly 10-year cycle during the 1960s to the just over one-year cycle beginning in 1980. Although not identical, all of the cycles exhibit similar up-and-down patterns.

Some generalizations about business cycles are useful:

- Expansions generally last longer than contractions. Since World War II, expansions have lasted about four times as long as contractions.
- Both real GNP and inflation generally show similar cyclical patterns.
- Business cycles have averaged about 50 months in length, but there is a lot of variability in the length of these cycles.
- Not all of the ups and downs in the economy are officially designated as business cycles.

Figure 2.1
Business Cycles in the United States Since 1870

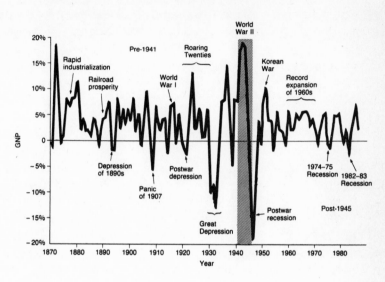

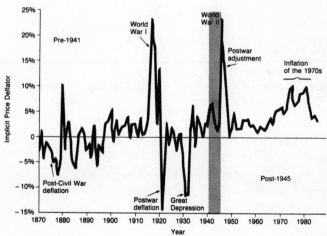

Source: Based on William J. Baumol and Alan S. Blinder, *Economic Principles and Policies*, San Diego, Calif.: Harcourt Brace Javanovich Publishers, 1988.

Exhibit 2.1
Measures of Economic Activity

It is not easy to define precisely the term *economic activity*. Economic activity has many dimensions. This circular flow diagram illustrates very

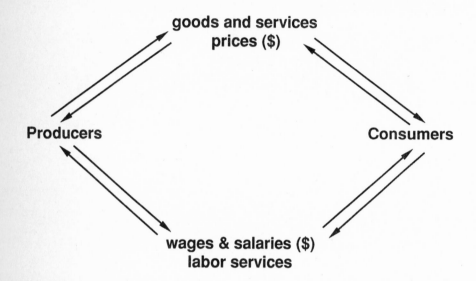

simply how our economy works. Producers produce final goods and services using consumers' labor. Consumers consume goods and services with the wages and salaries they earn from producers. This exchange occurs in a circular fashion.

Economic activity can be measured from either the upper or the lower portion of the circular flow. If economic activity is viewed from the goods and services side, gross national product (GNP) and inflation are good measures. If viewed from the perspective of labor and their earnings, wages and salaries and employment levels are good measures of economic activity. Changes in any of these four measures of economic activity over time show similar cyclical patterns.

A vital element of the economy is not shown in this simple circular flow—the banking system. Money is important in an economy because it makes transactions between producers and consumers more efficient. Can you imagine living in a barter economy? Borrowing and lending money influences interest rates. Changes in interest rates influence many business decisions.

Exhibit 2.2
Various Types of Business Cycles

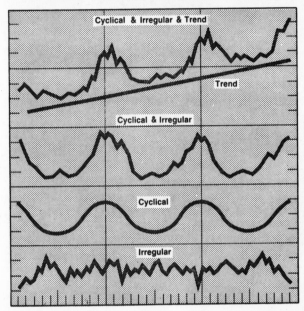

Source: Albert T. Sommers, *The U.S. Economy Demystified*, Lexington, Mass.: Lexington Books, 1988.

The official dates of the peaks and troughs of recent U.S. business cycles are listed in Table 2.1. These dates have been designated by the National Bureau of Economic Research (NBER). A brief history of NBER's involvement with business cycles is in Exhibit 2.3.

Dating peaks and troughs is an after-the-fact exercise. NBER researchers look at many statistics in order to date precisely when an expansion or contraction began or ended.

Interest rates are an important cyclical variable, as I explained in the previous chapter. However, interest rates are not a good measure of economic activity. They represent the price of borrowing money. Changes in interest rates are a response to the cycle, that is to actual or anticipated changes in aggregate demand or in macroeconomic policies.

Table 2.1
Turning Points in Economic Activity in the United States Since 1870

Trough	Peak	Duration of Contraction	Duration of Expansion
Dec. 1870	Oct. 1873	18	34
Mar. 1879	Mar. 1882	65	36
May 1885	Mar. 1887	38	22
Apr. 1888	July 1890	13	27
May 1891	Jan 1893	10	20
June 1894	Dec. 1895	17	18
June 1897	June 1899	18	24
Dec. 1900	Sept. 1902	18	21
Aug. 1904	May 1907	23	33
June 1908	Jan. 1910	13	19
Jan. 1912	Jan. 1913	24	12
Dec. 1914	Aug. 1918	23	44
Mar. 1919	Jan. 1920	7	10
July 1921	May 1923	18	22
July 1924	Oct. 1926	14	27
Nov. 1927	Aug. 1929	13	21
Mar. 1933	May 1937	43	50
June 1938	Feb. 1945	13	80
Oct. 1945	Nov. 1948	8	37
Oct. 1949	July 1953	11	45
May 1954	Aug. 1957	10	39
Apr. 1958	Apr. 1960	8	24
Feb. 1961	Dec. 1969	10	106
Nov. 1970	Nov. 1973	11	36
Mar. 1975	Jan. 1980	16	58
July 1980	July 1981	6	12
Nov. 1982	—	16	—

Source: Geoffrey H. Moore, *Business Cycles, Inflation, and Forecasting*, Cambridge, Mass.: Ballinger, 1983.

Exhibit 2.3
NBER's Business Cycle Research

The U.S. economy began to recover from the Great Depression in early 1933 and this recovery lasted just over four years. In May 1937, the economy went into a recession. Then Secretary of Treasury Henry Morgenthau, Jr., remembering the 1929–1933 period and being concerned about the future health of the country, asked the National Bureau of Economic Research (NBER) to study the cyclical nature of our economy and to develop indices to predict when the 1937 recession would end. NBER was, and still is, a private organization with a primary research interest in business cycles.

Secretary Morgenthau's charge was accepted by the Bureau's director, Wesley C. Mitchell. Assisted by Arthur F. Burns (who later became Chairman of the Federal Reserve Board, 1970–1978), the project had two major accomplishments: the development of the NBER indices of economic activity and the practice of NBER dating peaks and troughs of business cycles.

In my opinion, a third accomplishment was the development of a useful definition of business cycles. Burns and Mitchell formulated the following definition in 1946:

Business cycles are a type of fluctuation found in the aggregate economic activity of nations that organize their work mainly in business enterprises: a cycle consists of expansions occurring at about the same time in many economic activities, followed by similarly general recessions, contractions, and revivals which merge into the expansion phase of the next cycle; this sequence of changes is recurrent but not periodic; in duration business cycles vary from more than one year to ten to twelve years; they are not divisible into shorter cycles of similar character with amplitudes approximately their own.

This definition has influenced the definition used today. The U.S. Department of Commerce publishes the following definition in its *Business Conditions Digest:*

Exhibit 2.3 (continued)

Business cycles have been defined as sequences of expansion and contraction in various economic processes that show up as major fluctuations in aggregate economic activity—that is, in comprehensive measures of production, employment, income, and trade. While recurrent and pervasive, business cycles of historical experience have been definitely nonperiodic and have varied greatly in duration and intensity, reflecting changes in economic systems, conditions, policies, and outside disturbances.

It is important to remember that the business cycles shown in the diagrams in Figure 2.1 reflect not only natural swings in economic activity, but also the results of predetermined macroeconomic policies. One goal of macroeconomic policy is to dampen business cycles. If such policies were never implemented, these business cycles might be even more pronounced.

DO BUSINESS CYCLES OCCUR IN OTHER COUNTRIES?

Yes they do. Ups and downs in economic activity occur in every country. Many people think that the economic conditions in the United States drive the economies in the rest of the world. That may have been true to some degree during the post–World War I and World War II periods, but it is not true today.

A hallmark of modern history is the global nature of economic activity. Other countries are more technologically advanced and more productive today than ever before. Just look at the prominence of Japan and the growing competition from the rest of the world. As a result, goods and services are traded daily and the competition is keen. Because markets are worldwide, business cycles in one country are related to business cycles in other countries. This is especially true among industrialized nations. However, because economies have independent macroeconomic policies, their business cycles are not identical.

The pattern of inflation rate changes in the United States and in six other industrialized countries are illustrated in Figure 2.2. Clearly, rates of change slow down in recession periods (shaded areas). Business cycles over the past 20 years have been similar (but not identical) among the United States and Japan, West Germany, France, the United Kingdom, Italy, and Canada. As the European Community solidifies its trade relationships, business cycles among those countries will become more similar. Also, as the Pacific Rim economies develop, business cycles in such countries as Korea will begin to mirror those in Japan and the United States.

THE MANAGER'S VIEWPOINT

For the most part, corporate America realizes how similar businesses are in other industrial nations. As reported in Table 2.2, well over 50 percent of the 70 presidents/CEOs interviewed responded that business cycles are very similar in other economies. It is interesting to note that the manufacturing and high-tech companies' executives were the most familiar with this similarity. Perhaps this emphasizes the growing competitive pressures on these companies, compared to those in the service sector.

Figure 2.2
International Comparisons of Inflation Rates:
Annual Percentage Changes, 1977–Present

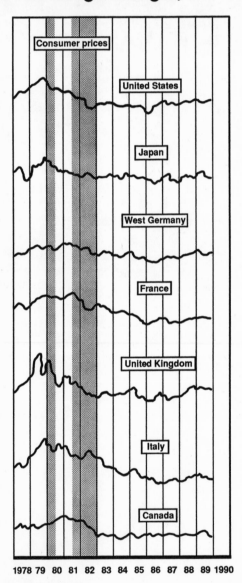

Source: *Business Conditions Digest.*

Table 2.2
How Familiar Managers Are with Business Cycles in Other Countries

Are business cycles in the United States similar to those in other industrialized countries?

Type of Company	Very Similar	Somewhat Similar	Not Very Similar	Not Similar at All
Manufacturing (40)	38	2	0	0
Service (15)	1	13	1	0
High Tech (15)	11	3	1	0

ACTION ITEMS

☞ Learn as much as you can about your customers. You should know what economic factors influence their buying behavior.

☞ With better knowledge about your customer base you will be able to predict more accurately the relationship between economywide swings and swings in the demand for your product.

☞ If you face international competition, follow the economic events in those countries, too. Their business cycles may directly affect your domestic sales and may indirectly affect your suppliers' activities.

CHAPTER 3
Factors Influencing Business Cycles

Every cause produces more than one effect.

Herbert Spencer

Business cycles are generally caused by fluctuations in aggregate demand. These fluctuations are determined by the collective behavior of households, companies, and the government. Because of the complexity of the relationships between these three groups, business cycles can be predicted only with a degree of accuracy.

Most of us naturally think in terms of cause and effect. If this happens, then that will happen; if this can be prevented, then that will not happen.

While this type of logic is ingrained in each of us from childhood—if you misbehave, then . . . —it does not apply equally well when trying to understand the causes or timing of business cycles. The topic is too complex.

When dealing with the collective behavior of all participants in the economy, a change in only one factor can have many ramifications. There are simply so many actors and so many possible interactions that prediction is more an art than a science. This being the case does not, however, nullify the importance of trying to anticipate change.

WHY ARE THERE BUSINESS CYCLES?

Although business cycles have complex roots, I want to rely on some simple explanations about why we have business cycles. Simple as these explanations are, they will provide you with a useful foundation for appreciating both the complexity of cycles and the importance of being able to anticipate them.

I defined business cycles in Chapter 1 in terms of alternating periods of expansion and contraction in economic activity. I also discussed in Chapter 2 two traditional measures of economic activity—real GNP and the inflation rate.

The supply and demand diagram in Figure 3.1 is one useful device for explaining why there are business cycles. In that diagram the upward sloping line represents aggregate supply (AgS) and the downward sloping line represents aggregate demand (AgD). The current level of GNP is represented at the intersection of AgS and AgD, noted by GNP*, and the current average price level is noted by P*.

Figure 3.1
Aggregate Supply and Demand

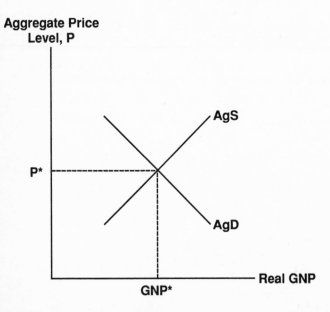

Aggregate supply is, using some economic terminology, an upward sloping function of prices. This phrase means that the aggregate supply of goods and services by all producers in the economy increases as prices increase. Simply put, producers supply more at higher prices than at lower prices.

Aggregate demand is a downward sloping function of prices. This means that more goods and services are purchased by customers at lower prices than at higher prices. Simply put, customers demand more at lower prices than at higher prices.

There are business cycles because aggregate supply and aggregate demand change. Because aggregate supply generally changes only as a result of major technological breakthroughs or random shocks (like an unexpected oil embargo), I will specifically focus only on the more frequently occurring changes in aggregate demand.

Periodic fluctuations in aggregate demand cause real GNP and interest rates to move cyclically. Recall that these movements were illustrated and called business cycles in Figure 2.1.

When aggregate demand increases, real GNP increases and the price level increases. You can see this in the upper diagram in Figure 3.2. The AgD curve shifts to the right. This happens in an expansion. Just the opposite happens when aggregate demand decreases. In the lower diagram in Figure 3.2, the AgD curve shifts to the left. This is what happens in a contraction. Increases and decreases in aggregate demand (and supply) cause business cycles.

Some of the early theories and explanations for changes in aggregate demand, and thus business cycles, are fascinating. I have capsulized several of these in Exhibit 3.1.

WHY DOES AGGREGATE DEMAND CHANGE?

There are four components to GNP:

- consumption (C)
- investment (I)
- government purchases (G)
- net exports (NX)

Figure 3.2
Changes in Aggregate Demand

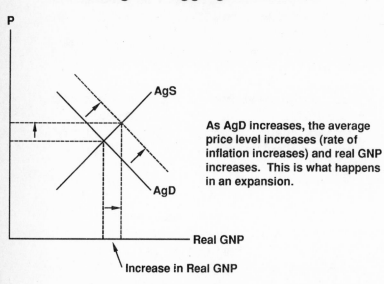

As AgD increases, the average price level increases (rate of inflation increases) and real GNP increases. This is what happens in an expansion.

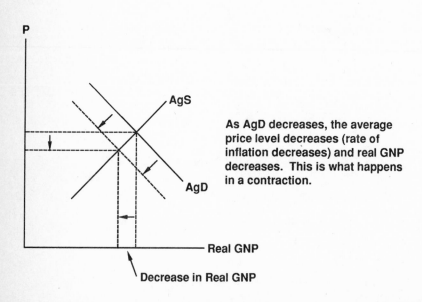

As AgD decreases, the average price level decreases (rate of inflation decreases) and real GNP decreases. This is what happens in a contraction.

Exhibit 3.1
Some Economic Theories of Business Cycles

Why the economy has ups and downs has long puzzled economists. Adam Smith and Thomas Malthus (late 1700s) saw business cycles as the result of population changes. When agricultural harvests were good, health improved, infant mortality decreased, and longevity increased. Economic activity increased as well. As populations grew, congestion caused conflict and resources became scarce. The population decreased in response, as did the economy.

William Jevons hypothesized in the mid-1870s that sunspots caused business cycles. His logic was: sunspots affected weather, weather changes affected agricultural production, changes in agricultural production affected the economy; therefore, sunspots caused economic activity to change.

Joseph Schumpeter, writing in the early 1900s, stressed the role of innovation in business cycles. As entrepreneurs innovated, new products, companies, and industries emerged. When economic activity expanded, the rate of innovation declined as entrepreneurs waited for consumers' demands for new products to increase again. These reactions influenced economic activity in a cyclical fashion.

The more modern theories of business cycles, often called classical theories, emphasize that business cycles are the natural response of a self-regulating economy to changes. While public policies can stimulate or dampen cycles to some degree, there remains a natural cyclical element which magnifies imperfect expectations on the part of buyers and sellers.

so there are four reasons why aggregate demand might change.

One way to write the relationship between GNP and these components is:

$$GNP = C + I + G + NX.$$

Obviously, GNP will increase when any one of these components increases, or when the net effect from several changes is positive. I will discuss each of these individually, but the GNP = C + I + G + NX relationship is also described schematically in Exhibit 3.2.

Consumption

Consumption expenditures change in response to increases and decreases in individuals' demands for goods and services. These changes are influenced by individuals' income and their expectations about the future rate of inflation. Aggregate income, in turn, is related to the economy's overall level of employment and to tax policies. When taxes increase, individuals have less income to spend. When there are expectations that inflation will increase in the future, individuals frequently purchase now to avoid higher prices in the future. These relationships are illustrated in Figure 3.3. This figure also shows how easy it is for consumption, and hence GNP, to increase or decrease in a spiraling fashion.

Exhibit 3.2
The Components of Aggregate Demand and Factors Influencing Them

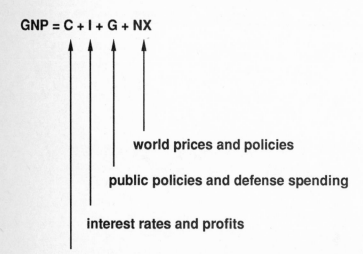

GNP = C + I + G + NX

world prices and policies

public policies and defense spending

interest rates and profits

income, employment levels, taxes, and expected inflation

Figure 3.3
Spiraling Effects on Consumption

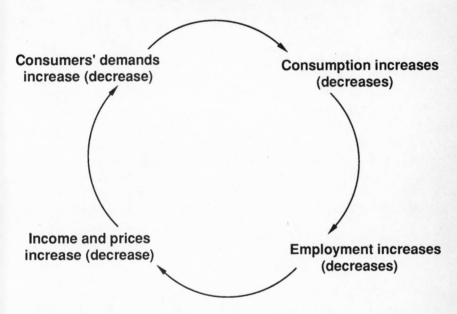

Investment

Companies' investments in plant and equipment depend on two things: current and future interest rates, and profit. Financing costs depend directly on interest rates, and are a prime factor when considering building a new plant or purchasing new equipment. These decisions are also influenced by current and expected profit. Profit is one signal that consumers are buying your products. Therefore, an expansion may be needed in order to continue to meet customer demand. Whereas profit reflects consumer satisfaction with your products, interest rates are determined primarily by the Federal Reserve system's macroeconomic monetary policies.

Government Purchases

The government buys goods and services primarily in response to changes in its need to provide services like defense. But over the next decades large expenditures will be needed to repair our nation's infrastructure (e.g., roads and bridges) and to improve public education. Government purchases will certainly increase. My guess is that taxes will also increase in order to finance these expenditures.

Net Exports

Total exports minus total imports equals net exports. The level of exports and imports depends on two things. One is the price of U.S. goods and services compared to those in foreign countries. When foreign-made products cost less than U.S.-made products, imports increase. The other is the extent to which the government imposes tariffs and quotas. These policy actions have a direct impact on the ability of companies to import or export.

So, there are eight underlying factors which influence business cycles:

- consumers' income
- the level of employment
- tax policies
- expectations about future inflation
- current and future interest rates
- monetary policies
- profit levels
- domestic and international governmental trade policies.

A more complete explanation of the factors affecting aggregate supply and demand is in Appendix A.2.

CAN BUSINESS CYCLES BE PREDICTED?

Yes they can . . . to a degree. Such an answer should not seem surprising to you in light of all the caveats I have given in this chapter. The workings of the economy are complicated! As the epigram at the beginning of this chapter says, every action in an economy has many ramifications. Also, there are many things than can change in the economy to cause GNP to change. Such events not only include policy actions—such as tax changes, monetary policies, industrial policies, public spending programs, and much more—but also include changes in the expectations of individuals. It is amazing that with all of these complex interactions, there still remains some degree of predictability about where the economy is going. You must understand and anticipate this degree of predictability and rely on it as you effectively manage.

As you will see in the next section of this book, many forecasters try to predict the future of our economy. In fact, the government is also involved in this activity. They publish several series of economic indicators designed to predict turns in the business cycle.

Neither forecasters nor published statistics are perfect predictors of the future. However, this is not a good reason to ignore what information there is. Recall the Bill Lawrence situation. His lack of effort cost his company a significant amount of money. You, as an astute business person, should make use of the available information, understand its limitations, and then make as informed a decision as possible.

THE MANAGER'S VIEWPOINT

It is pretty clear from the presidents/CEOs I interviewed, that they pay closer attention to changes in customers' tastes than to government policy when looking toward the future. See Table 3.1. This is not surprising. I think we all pay closer attention to those things we can influence than we do to those we cannot. Few companies, if any, have the political clout to direct policy. But most companies rely on their marketing efforts to influence customers' tastes, whether the customer is a final consumer or another manufacturer.

Keeping this in mind, the vast majority of company presidents/CEOs think that business cycles can be predicted only to a limited degree. And, they believe that it is important to do so. At best, they think that the job they are doing is average.

Table 3.1
Managers' Views on Factors Influencing
the Business Cycle

Are changes in government policies more or less important than changes in customers' tastes when predicting business cycles?

Type of Company	More Important	Less Important
Manufacturing (40)	9	31
Service (15)	3	12
High Tech (15)	4	11

How well can business cycles be predicted?

Type of Company	Very Well	To a Limited Degree	Very Poorly
Manufacturing (40)	0	38	2
Service (15)	0	14	1
High Tech (15)	0	12	3

Is it important to try to predict business cycles?

Type of Company	Yes	No
Manufacturing (40)	40	0
Service (15)	15	0
High Tech (15)	15	0

Table 3.1 (continued)

Grade your company's efforts at anticipating business cycle movements and using this information in business planning.

Type of Company	A	B	C	D	F
Manufacturing (40)	1	7	28	4	0
Service (15)	0	3	11	1	0
High Tech (15)	1	0	8	6	0

Are you trying to improve upon this grade?

Type of Company	Yes	No
Manufacturing (40)	40	0
Service (15)	15	0
High Tech (15)	14	1

ACTION ITEMS

☞ Learn about the relationship between changes in factors affecting the business cycle and those affecting your company. If you are a top executive, provide seminars and training programs to keep your middle managers up to date on how the economy works and its trends.

☞ Make efforts to anticipate changes in factors which affect your company's demand. Instill in your subordinates the importance of anticipating new opportunities. Prepare yourself to be receptive to their suggestions.

SECTION 2
The Nature of
Economic Indicators

CHAPTER 4
Economic Indicators: What Are They?

A magician cannot produce a rabbit unless it is already in
. . . his hat. In the same way, surprises in the business
environment almost never emerge without warning.

Pierre Wack
Royal Dutch/Shell

Economic indicators signal changes in economic activity. Indicators fall into three categories: leading indicators, coincident indicators, and lagging indicators. The activities measured by each indicator are related because market activities in the economy are related.

Recall Bill Lawrence's situation from Chapter 1. He expected the economy to be growing for the next 12 to 18 months when he made his financial commitment to purchase $600,000 of electronic component parts. However, he miscalculated it. But, how could he have known what was going to happen? What is a manager to do? Are managers expected to be magicians and pull forecasts out of their hats?

WHAT IS AN ECONOMIC INDICATOR?

You have certainly heard of economic indicators. You can hardly go a day without reading about them or seeing reports on the news concerning this one going up or that one going down. An economic indicator is a series of data which corresponds to movements in economic activity. Simply put, it is a signal of economic change.

There are many economic indicators, but those best known and most widely publicized are constructed by the Bureau of Economic Analysis (BEA), with the assistance of the National Bureau of Economic Research (NBER). They were previously published in *Business Conditions Digest* and are now published in the *Survey of Current Business*. BEA calls their indicators cyclical indicators (for obvious reasons):

> One of the techniques developed in business cycle research and widely used as a tool for analyzing current economic conditions and prospects is the cyclical indicators approach. This approach identifies certain economic time series as tending to lead, coincide with or lag behind the broad movements in aggregate economic activity.

The general notion behind an economic indicator is rather straightforward. The circular flow diagram from Exhibit 2.1, reproduced here in Figure 4.1, illustrates what an economic indicator is all about. The activities of producers and consumers, felt through markets, influence economic activity as measured in terms of goods and services (GNP) and price changes (inflation). Let me emphasize how simple this explanation is. There are actually more aggregate markets in the economy which influence economic activity than just the labor market or the final goods and services (output) market. There is a money market, a credit market, and so on.

THREE CATEGORIES OF ECONOMIC INDICATORS

Economic indicators fall into three broad categories: leading indicators, coincident indicators, and lagging indicators. Although

Figure 4.1
What an Economic Indicator Is All About

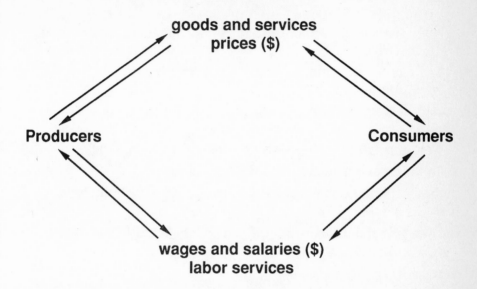

these are the categories used by the BEA, any economic indicator, government or not, must be one of these types. Any measure of economic activity must foretell, move with, or follow the cycle.

Leading Indicators

The BEA tracks eleven leading indicators of economic activity. They are listed in Table 4.1. Each reflects activity which foretells cyclical swings in the economy. For example, employers change the average weekly hours of their production and non-supervisory workers based on expectations (preliminary information from their customers) about future changes in demand. Similarly, unemployment claims increase before the economy officially turns down and decrease before the economy officially turns up. These and other indicators come from the NBER (see Exhibit 2.3).

The BEA also calculates a composite (average) index from these eleven indicators. The diagram in Figure 4.2 shows that this composite index turns ahead (shown by –) of the official business

Table 4.1
BEA's Eleven Leading Indicators of Economic Activity

1. Average weekly hours of production or non-supervisor workers, manufacturing.
2. Average weekly initial claims for unemployment insurance, state programs (inverted index).
3. Manufacturers' new orders, consumer goods, and materials industries.
4. Vendor performance—slower deliveries diffusion index.
5. Contracts and orders for plant and equipment.
6. New private housing units authorized by local building permits.
7. Change in manufacturers' unfilled orders, durable goods.
8. Change in sensitive materials prices.
9. Stock prices, 500 common stocks.
10. Money supply, M_2.
11. Index of consumer expectations.

cycle. Again, the shaded areas denote officially labeled recessions. This composite index has generally predicted an upturn in the business cycle fewer months ahead of time than it has predicted a downturn.

Leading economic indicators are what Bill Lawrence should have been watching.

Coincident Indicators

The four coincident indicators listed in Table 4.2 move with (coincide with) the business cycle. Whereas hours of production are a leading indicator, the number of employees hired is a coincident indicator. It seems logical that businesses adjust the hours of their employees before adjusting the actual number of employees in anticipation of a cyclical change in demand. Aggregate employment

Figure 4.2
BEA's Composite Index of Eleven Leading Indicators

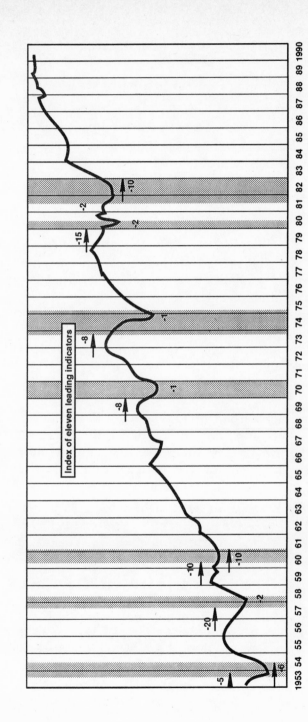

Source: *Business Conditions Digest.*

Table 4.2
BEA's Four Coincident Indicators of Economic Activity

1. Employees on nonagricultural payrolls.
2. Personal income less transfer payments.
3. Industrial production.
4. Manufacturing and trade sales.

changes are directly related to aggregate income, and income changes are directly related to aggregate sales. That is why all of these are coincident indicators.

The diagram in Figure 4.3 shows that the BEA's composite index of coincident indicators moves almost identically (noted by zeros) with the business cycle. It drops as a recession begins, and recovers immediately after.

Lagging Indicators

The seven indicators listed in Table 4.3 lag the economy's cyclical swings. See also the diagram in Figure 4.4; the plus signs indicate the lagging nature of this composite indicator. Note that labor costs are a lagging indicator. Recall that hours worked are a leading indicator and that number of employees is a coincident indicator. The logical relationship between these three activities underscores the systematic relationship that exists between markets in the economy.

ARE ECONOMIC INDICATORS RELATED TO EACH OTHER?

Economic indicators are indeed related to each other. In fact, as complex as the aggregate economy is, it does operate in a logical and systematic fashion. Activities in one market directly affect activities in other markets. (Refer again to Appendix A.2.)

I have already outlined how the labor market operates. Its workings explain why hours of production are a leading indicator,

Figure 4.3
BEA's Composite Index of Four Coincident Indicators

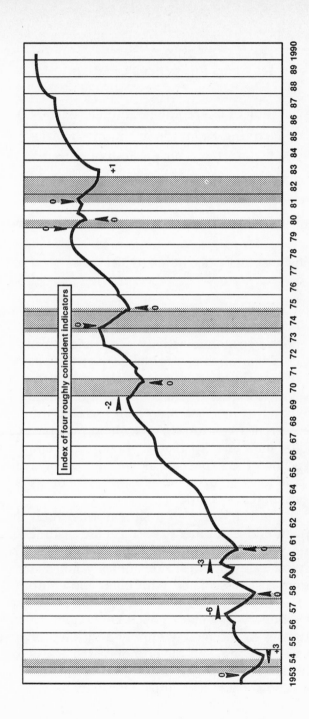

Source: *Business Conditions Digest.*

Table 4.3
BEA's Seven Lagging Indicators of Economic Activity

1. Average duration of unemployment (inverted index).
2. Ratio, manufacturing and trade inventories to sales.
3. Change in index of labor costs per unit of output.
4. Average prime rate charged by banks.
5. Commercial and industrial loans outstanding.
6. Ratio, consumer installment credit outstanding to personal income.
7. Change in consumer price index for services.

employment levels are a coincident indicator, and labor costs are a lagging indicator of economic activity. The diagram in Figure 4.5 shows how most businesses control labor over the business cycle. For example, when the economy is at the end of a contraction phase and managers expect (perhaps through the use of their own indicators) demand to increase, they will increase the number of hours of their current work force. As demand materializes and the economy enters into an expansion phase, new employees are hired. Finally, when the expansion is well underway, other firms begin to compete for workers, and as a result, labor costs go up. It is all very logical and systematic.

The money market works in a similar way. Both the money supply and plant and equipment contracts are leading indicators, and the prime rate of interest is a lagging indicator. When the money supply increases, interest rates quickly fall, thereby lowering the financing costs associated with plant and equipment. (This is the intent of an expansionary monetary policy—to lower interest rates. A contractionary monetary policy is intended to raise interest rates.) Increases in the money supply and lower interest rates spur consumer borrowing, and the economy then starts to turn up. Once an expansion is underway (motivated by this monetary policy), prices rise and consumers compete for loanable funds. Both of

Figure 4.4
BEA's Composite Index of Lagging Indicators

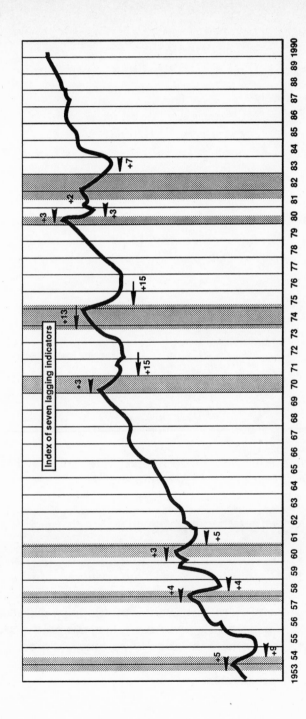

Source: *Business Conditions Digest.*

Figure 4.5
Relationship of Indicators to How the Labor Market Works

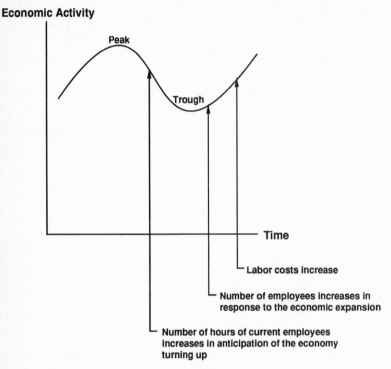

these effects compound to cause interest rates to rise. Therefore, the prime rate of interest lags the economy.

OTHER ECONOMIC INDICATORS

The indicators described above are governmental indicators, but any rate that leads, coincides, or lags the economy can be used as an economic indicator. Most managers have their own crystal balls for foretelling changes in economic activity. Not all industries move together, so aggregate indicators may be more useful to some managers than others in terms of helping to forecast industry demand. Aggregate indicators are nonetheless useful for anticipating economywide swings.

Most managers keep in close contact with their major customers and have a pulse on what is going on in their niche of the economy. Sales people regularly report to upper management trends that they perceive, and upper management generally acts accordingly. This is a good practice; customer behavior is one key variable to predict.

At the local level, Chambers of Commerce report regularly business confidence indices and local vacancy rates to give some signal to the business population as to what is going on in the community.

Whichever indices are used, and more than one should be used, they still either lead, move with, or lag the business cycle.

THE MANAGER'S VIEWPOINT

The numbers in Table 4.4 tell a fairly consistent story. Managers of manufacturing companies, high-tech or otherwise, pay close attention to where the economy is expected to go. This seems logical because they need lead time to adjust their operations. In contrast, managers in the service sector are relatively more interested in what is going on now. To these business leaders coincident indicators are the most important.

Table 4.4
Economic Indicators and Managerial Decisions

Which of the official economic indicators do you pay the most attention to when making an important business decision?

Type of Company	Leading	Coincident	Lagging
Manufacturing (40)	39	1	0
Service (15)	4	11	0
High Tech (15)	15	0	0

ACTION ITEMS

☞ Look for economic indicators which are specific to your company. Do you notice any relationships between changes in either economy-wide variables or industry-specific variables and changes in your sales? Have someone in your company monitor such relationships. Be sure to explain to them why this job is important.

☞ If your suppliers are directly affected by business cycle fluctuations, plan accordingly. Expect delivery delays and perhaps price increases when the economy expands and the demand for their products increases. Plan accordingly.

CHAPTER 5
Economic Indicators: Where Are They?

Knowledge is of two kinds: we know a subject ourselves,
or we know where we can find information upon it.

James Boswell

Economic indicators are readily available. They are published in easy to access places and they are regularly reported in the news. Managers should pay attention to these announcements and to trends in these indicators.

I have suggested in the previous chapters that Bill Lawrence's miscalculation of the state of the economy *might have*—not necessarily *could have*—been prevented. He made a very important financial decision based on limited information about what his company's sales would do over the next year to year-and-a-half, and based on no information about the state of the economy. What should he have done? Should he, or should any manager, keep abreast of current economic trends? Yes, it really is not that difficult or time consuming. As Bill's case illustrates, failing to keep up with economic trends may have disastrous results.

WHERE DO I LOOK FOR ECONOMIC INDICATORS?

The formal economic indicators discussed in Chapter 4—the government leading, coincident, and lagging indicators—are put together by government agencies and are released in public documents. They previously appeared in the Department of Commerce's monthly publication, *Business Conditions Digest*. Now, they appear in the *Survey of Current Business*. These publications are generally kept in the reference section of public libraries and in the government documents section of college and university libraries. They can be purchased from the Government Printing Office, but I suggest to most managers that these publications are probably too intricate for their general forecasting purposes. The diagrams in Chapter 4 came from *Business Conditions Digest*.

Many of the Federal Reserve Banks' publications are very useful, and often are free for the asking. They are an excellent resource for managers concerned about economic trends. These publications vary in their coverage and readability. I have listed some in Exhibit 5.1, along with the relevant mailing addresses.

One monthly Federal Reserve publication that I think all managers should scan on a regular basis is *Economic Trends* (Federal Reserve Bank of Cleveland). It provides a readable perspective on all aspects of the domestic economy, and it complements this perspective with easy to understand charts and diagrams.

Another excellent resource is *National Economic Trends* (Federal Reserve Bank of St. Louis). It contains a more detailed collection of charts and tables, and is very helpful for the manager who calculates trends and past changes in economic variables.

In addition to these two publications, many of the business-oriented popular press magazines publish either their own indices of economic activity or related government statistics. For example, the Forbes Index, published in *Forbes,* is an average index based on eight key economic indicators: the Department of Labor's consumer price index, the Department of Commerce's manufacturers' new orders and inventories, the Federal Reserve Board's industrial production index, the Department of Commerce's new housing starts, the Department of Commerce's personal income series, the Department of Labor's new unemployment claims, the Depart-

Exhibit 5.1
Selected Federal Reserve Bank Publications

Bank	*Publication*
Federal Reserve Bank of Boston 600 Atlantic Avenue Boston, MA 02183-0999	*New England Economic Indicators*
Federal Reserve Bank of Philadelphia Box 66 Philadelphia, PA 19105-0066	*Business Outlook Survey* *Mid-Atlantic Manufacturing Index* *Quarterly Regional Report*
Federal Reserve Bank of Richmond P.O. Box 27622 Richmond, VA 23261-7622	*District Economic Activity* *in Cross Sections*
Federal Reserve Bank of Atlanta P.O. Box 1731 Atlanta, GA 30301-1731	*Economic Update* *Financial Update* *Regional Update*
Federal Reserve Bank of Chicago Box 834 Chicago, IL 60609-0834	*Chicago Fed Letter* *Economic Perspective*
Federal Reserve Bank of Minneapolis 250 Marquette Avenue Minneapolis, MN 55401-2117	*District Economic Conditions*
Federal Reserve Bank of Kansas City Federal Reserve Station Kansas City, MO 64198-0001	*Financial Letter* *Economic Review*
Federal Reserve Bank of San Francisco P.O. Box 7702 San Francisco, CA 94120-7702	*FRBSF Weekly Letter*
Federal Reserve Bank of Cleveland PO Box 6387 Cleveland, OH 44101-1387	*Economic Trends* *Economic Commentary*
Federal Reserve Bank of St. Louis P.O. Box 442 St. Louis, MO 63166-0442	*National Economic Trends*

ment of Commerce's retail sales, and the Federal Reserve Board's consumer installment credit series.

Business Week also publishes its own leading index of economic activity, as well as other selected government indicators on production activity and monetary policy.

The Conference Board calculates a monthly index of consumer confidence based on a national survey of some 5,000 households. The index is reported widely, even in most local newspapers, upon its announcement at the beginning of each month. This confidence index has been fairly stable over recent years, as shown in Figure 5.1.

The Economist publishes a number of interesting statistics, such as changes in the money supply, interest rates, consumer prices, and GNP for the industrial nations of the world.

Figure 5.1
The Conference Board's Index of Consumer Confidence

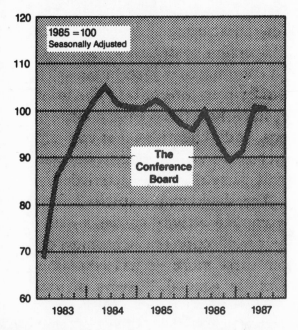

Source: Albert T. Sommers, *The U.S. Economy Demystified*, Lexington, Mass.: Lexington Books, 1988.

Most recently, the NBER developed a recession index which quantifies the probability of a recession beginning in X number of months. It is released regularly and is highly publicized.

There are also many other indices calculated and published by private sources, such as brokerage houses or consulting companies. In addition, most local Chambers of Commerce prepare indices of their local economy in order to assist local businesses with their planning activities.

WHEN DO I LOOK FOR ECONOMIC INDICATORS?

The formal government indices discussed in Chapter 4 are announced every month. Exhibit 5.2 is a calendar of a representative month. On the calendar are listed the approximate dates when many of these key indicators are released. With only one exception, these indicators refer to the activities of the previous month. The announcement dates will vary from month to month, but this calendar is a reasonable planning guide. *The Wall Street Journal* reports every Monday the indicators to be announced that week.

Generally, the news media reports these indices on the day they are released. People anticipate these releases. At least once a month you can read a report that the stock market went up or down in response to some change in one of these indices. This in itself is an indication that people take them seriously.

All but one of the indicators in Exhibit 5.2 relate to economic activity from the previous month. Gross National Product, GNP, is calculated and reported quarterly. However, estimates and revisions are reported monthly. For example, the advance estimate of first quarter GNP is announced in April, the preliminary estimate of first quarter GNP is then announced in May, and the revised estimate of first quarter GNP is finally released in June. In July, the advance estimate of second quarter GNP is announced, and so on.

A more detailed accounting of 17 common groups of indicators is in Exhibit 5.3.

I think it is a good practice for top management to collect information about the economy and their industry, and then route it through key personnel in all functional areas. This information

Exhibit 5.2
Approximate Dates When Economic Indicators
Are Released

Sunday	Monday	Tuesday	Wednesday	Thursday	Friday	Saturday
	1 BOC New Family Houses Sold, for Sale	2 CB Consumer Confidence Index	3	4	5 BLS Employment Report	6
7	8	9	10	11	12 BOC Retail Sales	13
14	15 FRB Production and Capacity Utilization Index	16	17	18	19 BLS Consumer Price Index	20
21	22	23	24	25 BEA GNP Estimate	26 BEA Personal Income and Expenditure	27
28	29	30 BEA Composite Indices	31			

BOC: Bureau of the Census
CB: Conference Board
BLS: Bureau of Labor Statistics
FRB: Federal Reserve Board
BEA: Bureau of Economic Analysis

Exhibit 5.3
Economic Indicators and Related Reference Material

The following provides the reader with an overview of 17 common groups of economic indicators as well as the sources for locating these data.

Employment-household and nonfarm payroll, unemployment rates, and average weekly hours and earnings, by the U.S. Department of Labor. Each monthly *News, The Employment Situation* put out by the Bureau of labor Statistics contains numerous explanatory notes. The *BLS Handbook of Methods, 1988,* goes into greater detail on the methodologies and gives further technical references. The Labor Department's monthly publication, *Employment and Earnings,* contains some of the same information as *The BLS Handbook of Methods,* See also *Handbook of Cyclical Indicators, 1984* (BEA) and *Monthly Labor Review,* "Notes on Current Labor Statistics." The Labor Department's *Monthly Labor Review* also publishes these data series but with a slightly longer lag than the *News.* Recommended reading includes "Comparing Employment Estimates from Household and Payroll Surveys," by Gloria P. Green, *Monthly Labor Review,* December 1969, pp. 9-20.

Auto Sales-Unit New, as released by the U.S. Department of Commerce in *Survey of Current Business,* section 5-32. the Bureau of Economic Analysis (BEA) collects data primarily from the Motor Vehicle Manufacturers' Association (MVMA), Detroit, Michigan (for domestic sales), and also from *Ward's Automotive Reports* (for import sales). Data essentially are reported by manufacturers' individual marketing sections and compiled by MVMA and Ward's. No written documentation is available. the BEA seasonally adjusts the data.

Retail Sales and Inventories, by the U.S. Department of Commerce. Basic information on data is found in each monthly issue of *Monthly Retail Trade,* published by the U.S. Department of Commerce, Bureau of the Census. Only retail sales data appear in the earlier release, *Advance Retail Sales,* also published by the Bureau. See also "Retail Sales: A Primer," by R. Mark Rogers, *Economic Review,* Federal Reserve Bank of Atlanta, April 1985, pp. 28-33.

Industrial Production, by the Federal Reserve Board of Governors. Monthly data are in *Federal Reserve Statistical Release, G. 12.3, Industrial Production* and in *Federal Reserve Bulletin.* Brief explanatory notes are included. Details for the construction of the data can be found in *Industrial Production - 1986 Edition, With a Description of the Methodology,* which is published by the Board of Governors but is not an "annual" version of the monthly releases. Data are historical and in fine detail. This publication usually follows major benchmark revisions of the data. The latest edition also includes chapters on "Seasonal Adjustment," "Uses and Limitations of the Index," "History of the Index," and a "Glossary of Terms."

Capacity Utilization Rates, by the Federal Reserve Board of Governors. Monthly data are in *Federal Reserve Statistical Release, G.3, Capacity Utilization,* and in *Federal Reserve Bulletin.* Explanatory notes are generally minimal. Information on methodology can be found in a special article, "*Revised Federal Reserve Rates and Capacity Utilization,*" in the section, "Appendix: Methodology," *Federal Reserve Bulletin,* October 1985, pp. 760-766, by Richard D. Raddock. Other useful information can be found in: "New Federal Reserve Measures of Capacity and Capacity Utilization," *Federal Reserve Bulletin,* July 1983, pp. 515-521, by Ronald F. Rost; and "Capacity Utilization," by Marjorie H. Schnader in *The Handbook of Economics and Financial Measures,* edited by Fabozzi and Greenfield, Dow Jones-Irwin, Homewood, Illinois, 1984, pp. 74-104.

Gross National Product, by the U.S. Department of Commerce. Data are quarterly, but

Exhibit 5.3 (continued)

releases are monthly when revisions are included. The most commonly used publication for these reports is Commerce's monthly *Survey of Current Business.* Explanatory notes occur at irregular intervals. the July issues generally have revised data for the previous three calendar years. See the *National Income and Product Accounts of the United States, 1929-82: Statistical Tables* for historical data. the best overview is "GNP: An Overview of Source Data and Estimating Methods," by Carol S. Carson, *Survey of Current Business,* July 1987, pp. 103-126. This also has been published in the Methodology Paper Series by the BEA as MP-4 (GPO stock no. 003-010-00179-8). The article discusses components on both the product and income sides of the national income and product accounts. the latter section of the article contains an extensive "directory to information about GNP" which lists numerous previously published articles and papers on the sources for various GNP components. The BEA also has published several other methodology papers: *Introduction to National Economic Accounting* (1985), Methodology Paper Series MP-1 (GPO stock no. 003-010-00158-5); *Corporate Profits: Profits Before Tax, Profits Tax Liability, and Dividends* (1985), Methodology Paper Series MP-2 (GPO stock no. 003-010-00143-7); *Foreign Transactions* (1987), Methodology Paper Series MP-3 (GPO stock no. 003-010-00178-0); *Government Transactions* (1988), Methodology Paper Series MP-5 (GPO stock no. 003-010-00187-9). Forthcoming are papers on personal consumption expenditures (planned for 1989) and gross private domestic fixed investment.

Personal Income, Personal Consumption Expenditures, and Personal Taxes, by the U.S. Department of Commerce. Data are monthly and appear in the Commerce Department's *Survey of Current Business,* among other sources. The only major review of the information is "Monthly Estimates of Personal Income, Taxes, and Outlays," by James C. Byrnes et al., *Survey of Current*

Business, November 1979, pp. 18-38. Another useful article is "GNP: An Overview of Source Data and Estimating Methods," by Carol S. Carson, *Survey of Current Business,* July 1987, pp. 103-126. The BEA plans to publish a methodology paper in 1989 on personal consumption expenditures.

Manufactures' Shipments, Inventories, and Orders, by the U.S. Department of Commerce. Data are monthly and appear in Commerce's *Current Industrial Reports, Manufacturers' Shipments, Inventories and Orders,* otherwise known as "M3-1" reports. Information on derivation of the data is found in the annual reports under the same title as the monthly reports.

Housing Starts, by the U.S. Department of Commerce. Data are monthly and appear in *Current Construction Reports: Housing Starts,* otherwise known as "C20" reports. More extensive information on the derivation of data is found in each January issue when revised seasonal factors are released.

Housing Permits, by the U.S. Department of Commerce. Data are monthly and appear in *Current Construction Reports: Housing Units Authorized by Building Permits,* otherwise known as "C40" reports. More extensive information on the derivation of data is found in each April issue when revised seasonal factors are released. See also the January or April issues of *Current Construction Reports: Housing Starts.*

Construction Expenditures, by the U.S. Department of Commerce. Data are monthly and appear in *Current Construction Reports. Value of New Construction Put in Place,* otherwise known as "C30" reports. Information on methodology is found in each May issue when revised seasonal factors are released.

Producer Price Index, by the U.S. Department of Labor. Data are monthly and appear in the Labor Department's *Summary Data from the Producer Price Index News*

Exhibit 5.3 (continued)

Release and slightly later in *Monthly Labor Review.* This publication and more detailed data are found in Labor's monthly *Producer Price Indexes* publication. The *Monthly Labor Review* contains some explanatory material. More extensive notes can be found in the *BLS Handbook of Methods, 1988.*

Consumer Price Index, by the U.S. Department of Labor. Data are monthly and appear in the Labor Department's *Summary Data from the Consumer Price Index News Release* and slightly later in the *Monthly Labor Review.* More detailed data are found in Labor's monthly *CPI Detailed Report.* Some explanatory material can be found in this publication, *Summary Data,* and the *Monthly Labor Review.* More extensive information can be found in the *BLS Handbook of Methods, 1988.* See also *The Consumer Price Index: 1987 Revision,* Report 736 (Bureau of Labor Statistics, 1987) for information on the recent rebasing of the CPI to reflect 1982-84 expenditure patterns.

Merchandise Trade, Advance Report, by the U.S. Department of Commerce. Data are monthly and published in Census' *Highlights of U.S. Export and Import Trade.* Explanatory notes are included.

Wholesale Trade, by the U.S. Department of Commerce. Data are monthly and published in *Monthly Wholesale Trade.* Explanatory notes are in each issue.

New One-Family Houses Sold and for Sale, by the U.S. Department of Commerce. Data are monthly and are published in *Current Construction Reports, New One-Family Houses Sold and For Sale,* otherwise known as "C25" reports. More extensive information is found in the January issue when revised seasonal factors are released.

Index of Leading Indicators, by the U.S. Department of Commerce. Data are monthly and are published in *United States Department of Commerce News: Composite Indexes of Leading, Coincident, and Lagging Indicators* and also Commerce's *Business Conditions Digest.* Few explanatory notes appear in *News,* but extensive notes can be found in Commerce's *Handbook of Cyclical Indicators, 1984,* and in each issue of *Business Conditions Digest.* Numerous articles have been written in economic and financial literature about the index of leading indicators. See "A Descriptive Analysis of Economic Indicators," by Ronald A. Rath, *Review,* Federal Reserve bank of St. Louis, January 1985, pp. 14-24. Information on the latest changes in methodology and make-up if these indexes can be found in Marie P. Hertzberg and Barry A. Beckman, "Business Cycle Indicators: Revised Composite Indexes," *Survey of Current Business,* January 1984, pp. 23-28.

Source: R. Mark Rogers, "Tracking the Economy: Fundamentals for Understanding Data," *Economic Review,* Federal Reserve Bank of Atlanta, March/April 1989.

could be in the form of a formal memorandum or an informal cut-and-paste information sheet. The form is less important than the content. I wonder if things would have been different if Bill Lawrence regularly read a memorandum like this? Also, this effort by top management sends a positive signal to all concerned to be perceptive of change. I even know of several companies that ask for strategy suggestions based on their routing of this information. Suggestion boxes work at all levels.

THE MANAGER'S VIEWPOINT

I reported in Chapter 3 that many top executives think it is important to follow what the business cycle is doing (see Table 3.1). I also reported in Chapter 4 that they rely most heavily on leading indicators so as to anticipate change rather than to have to react to an unexpected change (see Table 4.4).

The information in Table 5.1 appears, at first glance, to be inconsistent with these previous remarks. Very few top executives follow the announcement of indicators each month. Those few who do are in the manufacturing sector.

Following up on this point with these executives, I learned that almost 70 percent of them have a designated individual who briefs them regularly on the state of the economy, as predicted by leading indicators. This relayed information is extensively used by the presidents/CEOs interviewed.

Table 5.1
Monday Homework for Managers: Do They Do It?

The Wall Street Journal *reports every Monday the economic indicators that are to be announced that week. Did you know this?*

Type of Company	Yes	No
Manufacturing (40)	11	29
Service (15)	1	14
High Tech (15)	3	12

Do you personally follow these announcements?

Type of Company	Yes	No
Manufacturing (40)	9	2
Service (15)	1	0
High Tech (15)	3	0

ACTION ITEMS

☞ Have information about economic indicators readily available for all key personnel.

☞ Encourage your managers and your staff to keep up to date on expected economywide trends. You do the same. Engage key personnel in informal dialogues about where the economy is going and what this means for the company now and in the future. Challenge them to think creatively and beyond their present boundaries of responsibility. When you do this, be supportive of whatever they say. Be ready to brainstorm.

☞ Think of ways to keep everyone in your company up to date on the state of the economy. Routing memoranda is useful, but put the names of top management on these memoranda, too. They should read the material, and it also sends a positive signal to everyone about the importance of the enclosed information.

CHAPTER 6
Economic Indicators: How to Use Them

I hope you'll keep in mind that economic forecasting is far from a perfect science. If recent history's any guide, the experts have some explaining to do about what they have told us had to happen but never did.

Ronald Reagan

Economic indicators should be interpreted carefully. They are a guide to understanding aggregate economic behavior, but do not necessarily predict what will happen in a particular industry or business. Managers not only need information about the economy as a whole, but also about their own consumers and their buying habits.

So far we have arrived at the conclusion that Bill Lawrence could have made a better investment decision for his electronics components company. He made a bad decision—but this happens to all of us from time to time. His error was he failed to anticipate when the demand for his company's product would soften. He misjudged a downturn in the business cycle, and that misjudgment hurt his company financially. Even if he had had information that the economy was likely to slow down in the next few months, what should he have done? What would you have done?

HOW DO I INTERPRET ECONOMIC INDICATORS?

The most important thing for anyone to remember when interpreting aggregate economic indicators is to be careful; in fact, be *very* careful. There are many things going on in our economy at the same time, and an economic indicator, even one researched and published by the federal government, only gives an *indication* of what may happen in the future. The second most important thing to remember is that these aggregate indicators *approximate* the overall activity of the economy. In fact, they are often revised several months after being released. Yet, even with this warning, some general information is often better than no information at all. Apparently, Bill Lawrence had no information at all.

There are a lot of professional economists who spend their careers interpreting economic indicators, especially leading economic indicators, and then forecasting what will happen in the future. Although they are all looking at the same data (and they were all probably taught economics and statistics out of similar textbooks), they frequently arrive at different conclusions.

It is not hard to find popular press publications which print articles on what is in store for the economy. These articles often show a table of a dozen or so predictions of prominent academic, bank, and government economists. The majority of the time the predictions of these groups are in agreement as to the direction the economy will follow, but there frequently is great diversity in opinions as to when a turning point is likely to occur. Nevertheless, it is my view that a consensus of professionals is generally more reliable than any one manager's guess as to what and when something will happen. One such collection of opinions (51 forecasters) is compiled by Robert Eggert and is called the Blue Chip consensus. It gets a lot of press when it is released.

Never try to interpret minor movements in a particular indicator (see Tables 4.1, 4.2, and 4.3). Such managerial myopia can prove dangerous and can often be financially costly. This advice not only holds when trying to understand the overall health of the economy, but also when trying to develop a business strategy for your own company. Get a big picture of the economy. One tree may fall in a storm, but the forest may be fine. If anything, I suggest that you:

- pay attention to the composite index of leading economic indicators and to a consensus as to what that index means
- follow reports on GNP and the consumer price index to see how accurate these predictions are.

A good rule of thumb is that if the composite index of leading economic indicators moves in the same direction for three consecutive months, then a cyclical trend is imminent. Learned people disagree with me on this. For example, Robert Hall of the NBER believes that it is unreliable to look at the number of quarters the economy has moved in the same direction in order to predict a recession, but rather to look at what he calls the "three Ds"—depth, dispersion, and duration—before making the call. Others adhere to a rule of two quarters of similar movement.

Some hypothetical values of leading indicators for a year are listed in Table 6.1. These indicators, like most, are indexed to a base year. That is why they are called indices. These hypothetical data are indexed to 1982, as is common: 1982 equals 100. If this index were 104.3 in 1983 it would mean activity increased 4.3 percent over that year. In the table the value of the indicator is 144.2 in January (J), which means this hypothetical index has increased 44.2 percent since 1982.

Consider the hypothetical monthly series of leading indicators listed under the heading of Situation A. I see no trend in these indicators and would not expect a turning point in the near future. To me it looks like the economy is rather stable.

Situation B seems to indicate an economy which will grow steadily into the next year. These leading indicators increased every month since September, but also, the overall trend is upward for the year. At worst, there is no evidence that the economy will turn down in the near future.

In comparison, Situation C predicts an upcoming swing in economic activity. This series suggests that a trough may occur in summer or fall of this year, with an upward swing thereafter. Re-

Table 6.1
Hypothetical Values of Leading Economic Indicators
(1982=100)

Month	Situation A	Situation B	Situation C	Situation D
J	144.2	144.2	144.1	144.2
F	144.3	144.2	144.2	144.4
M	144.1	144.4	144.1	144.6
A	144.6	144.3	144.1	144.1
M	144.5	144.5	144.1	144.0
J	144.7	144.5	144.4	144.0
J	144.5	144.6	144.6	143.8
A	144.3	144.8	144.7	143.9
S	144.4	144.7	144.8	143.8
O	144.3	144.9	144.9	143.7
N	144.5	145.1	145.0	143.2
D	144.7	145.2	145.2	143.2

member that these are leading indicators. They turn ahead of the economy. The turn in the indices in March/April suggests that the economy may do the same thing in the near future.

Situation D is an example of an economy that is likely to turn down, hitting its peak perhaps in late summer and then declining. My guess is that these data would be like the ones available had Bill Lawrence done his homework. But, we all know all about Monday morning quarterbacks.

Although Situations C and D suggest possible turns in economic activity, it may be the case that neither would be defined by the NBER researchers as an official turning point. The best that a manager can do when monitoring such series of leading economic indicators is to get an *indication* for which way the economy is tending, rather than how pronounced that trend may be.

The U.S. economy in late 1989 and early 1990 illustrated this point very well. Leading indicators suggested that the economy was sluggish, but no one knew for sure if there would be a period of slow growth, a period of decline into a recession, or a period of stagnation leading the economy to what would then be called a soft landing. After the fact, maybe in 1991 or 1992, economists will have a better picture of where the economy was. This means that managers have to make important decisions only on the basis of suggestive information. Still, suggestive information may be better than no information at all. One thing was certain in late 1989/early 1990—no one was predicting a prolonged expansion.

WHAT HAPPENS OVER THE BUSINESS CYCLE?

The driving force behind swings in the business cycle generally is changes in aggregate demand. I have discussed this issue in previous chapters. Will changes in aggregate demand affect your particular business? Maybe so, but maybe not.

A lot of things happen over the business cycle. Look at Exhibit 6.1. When aggregate demand changes, prices change. Increases in aggregate demand fuel inflation and decreases curb it. So, the output market influences prices over the business cycle, and price changes influence other markets. The labor market and the money market work similarly.

To understand what happens over the cycle in more detail, you need to understand why aggregate demand changes in the first place, and then you need to understand what follows. Both pieces of information are important when making decisions.

Keep in mind throughout this explanation that I am referring to economywide trends. Employment in some industries may increase more or less than in other industries. Certain components of the consumer price index may increase more or less than others. It is not necessarily the case that all businesses' sales or profits are affected the same way in an expansion as in a contraction. It is the case that all businesses have to react alike when certain aggregate markets change. For example, interests rates are determined in an economywide credit market. When interest rates change, all companies are affected.

Aggregate demand will increase, say when an expansion begins, for several reasons. The demand of customers—households,

Exhibit 6.1
How Markets Work in the Economy

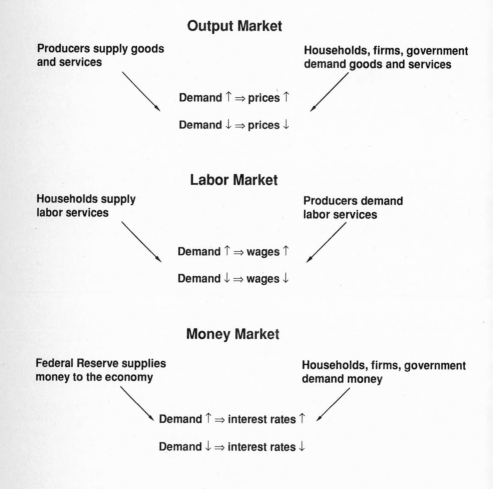

Output Market

Producers supply goods
and services

Households, firms, government
demand goods and services

Demand ↑ ⇒ prices ↑

Demand ↓ ⇒ prices ↓

Labor Market

Households supply
labor services

Producers demand
labor services

Demand ↑ ⇒ wages ↑

Demand ↓ ⇒ wages ↓

Money Market

Federal Reserve supplies
money to the economy

Households, firms, government
demand money

Demand ↑ ⇒ interest rates ↑

Demand ↓ ⇒ interest rates ↓

firms, and the government—may increase based on expectations of favorable things to come, or on economically and politically favorable changes in foreign countries. Expectations are a very important economic factor, but one that is extremely difficult to predict. Or, aggregate demand will increase if the government purposely stimulates the economy by reducing taxes and thus increasing disposable income and profit.

An increase in aggregate demand not only leads to higher prices and higher after tax profit, it also means that more goods and services will be produced. This in turn causes businesses to hire more workers—unemployment will fall—and to buy more materials. Buying more materials then increases employment in the materials-producing industries. Things snowball in such a situation.

As employment increases, so does aggregate income—when more people are employed, aggregate income is increased. When the income is spent, there is yet another increase in aggregate demand, and so on. This can create, as I said in an earlier chapter, a spiraling effect on prices.

To complete the illustration, as income increases some households demand more money (loanable funds) for purchases, and some companies demand more money for expansion and new construction. This increase in the aggregate demand for money brings about an increase in interest rates.

Refer back to Table 1.2. Just the reverse will take place when a contraction begins.

When a manager interprets a trend in a composite leading economic indicator to mean that the economy will soon enter into an expansion, he is in fact using those indicators to help himself forecast aggregate price movements, employment levels, wages, and interest rates. If you are such a manager, you must then determine how such aggregate changes will affect *your* own industry and business.

Had Bill Lawrence successfully watched how leading indicators were moving, he might have perceived (an entrepreneurial trait) that there was soon going to be a slowdown in the economy. And if a slowdown in the economy was likely, and if it would affect his company's sales, then he would have been wise to postpone purchasing component parts until there was an indication that demand was picking back up.

HOW RELIABLE ARE ECONOMIC INDICATORS?

Economic indicators, leading economic indicators in particular, are pretty good for predicting *aggregate* trends. However, there are at least three qualifications that I must add to this already general statement.

First, the government's composite index of leading economic indicators is a broad index of *total* economic activity. It is not an industry- or company-specific index. Trends may overstate or understate future activity in any one particular industry. This implies that you as a good manager must also know your customer base and have a very good understanding of what influences their buying habits. Some industries are insulated from cyclical changes in aggregate demand, such as the medical services industry. Also, some industries do better in downturns than in upturns, such as the home and automobile repair industries. Similarly, the profitability of companies is influenced as much by the managerial skills of its executives as by its sales. Companies do go bankrupt during expansionary times.

Second, even for a business in an industry where customer demand is not cyclical, chances are good that their suppliers' demand is cyclical. Managers must take this into account when scheduling deliveries, for example.

Third, my rule of thumb that three consecutive months determines a trend is only a rule of thumb. Imagine a situation when an indicator predicts a downturn in the business cycle. Unexpectedly, the government adopts an expansionary growth policy, maybe a tax cut, to thwart that trend. There is really no good way to predict if the government will intervene or to what extent. This means that you must also keep abreast of public policy—upcoming tax changes and weekly changes in the growth of the money supply—and its potential impact on the economy.

FORECASTING YOUR OWN DEMAND

Using published economic indicators is only a *first* step toward managing effectively over the business cycle. I do not recommend that any manager make major business decisions solely on the basis of their interpretation of a published indicator. It is equally important to develop your own indicators.

I have emphasized the importance of knowing about your customer base. I do not mean that you need to know every customer by name. But, such a personal touch is a very effective competitive strategy, especially in the service sector. I do mean that you should have a good profile of who buys your product and what motivates them. You also need to understand how changes in the economy can affect this profile.

Consulting companies are very willing and generally very able to provide, for a fee, such a customer profile. This may be a good investment to make. But do not lose sight of the fact that strategic management is not all numbers. It is, to a large degree, instinctive and I think that managers will manage more effectively if they take the time and effort to acquire customer-related information firsthand. This can be done through sales representatives, purchasing agents, surveys, or one-to-one conversations. Never be surprised at just how much a person will tell you either about themselves or what they want for their money.

You do not have to manage a small business to get to know your customers well. Some of the most successful conglomerates have divisional vice presidents interacting with their marketing people and purchasing agents on a regular basis. They also have representative customers as part of advisory groups. In some industries, especially the ones which compete in terms of new technology-based products, companies involve their customers in the design stage of a new product. I know of one manufacturing company president who attends annual sales conventions with his salespeople. This not only gives him the opportunity to interface with customers, but also it instills company loyalty and enthusiasm in the sales staff.

Even after you learn about your customer base, you must still exercise some care in forecasting their demand. Forecasting involves extrapolating future activity from past activity. And remember that extrapolating assumes the past will be duplicated in the future. See Figure 6.1. To be accurate, forecasting must incorporate as much information as possible about how future changes in the economy will differ from past changes.

Pretend your company is operating in 1991. You obviously know how your sales have increased in the past. If you expect the future to be like the past you could justifiably find a line to fit your historical data and extend it into the future. Such an extrapolation would predict in Figure 6.1 $1,000,000 in 1995.

However, why should the future be like the past? Perhaps economic policies designed to stimulate the economy have been successful. Perhaps your new products are more innovative than those of your competitors. If you think that your sales in the future will grow faster than in previous years, you might predict sales from a new forecasting line. If you did this, you would predict sales of $1,500,000 in 1995.

Figure 6.1
Forecasting Sales

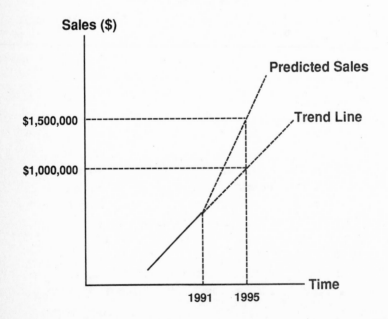

Some more sophisticated forecasting techniques are described in Appendix A.3. Although these techniques can get complicated, the basic notion of what they do is described by Figure 6.1.

THE MANAGER'S VIEWPOINT

Company-specific forecasting is an important complement to published economic indicators. As the data in Table 6.2 show, most companies, regardless of their industry, do some sort of in-house forecasting. Every president/CEO with whom I have consulted emphasized over and over to me that they insist their forecasters (usually in the marketing area) *first* learn about their customers and *then* begin to forecast their demand.

Interestingly, only the manufacturing companies rely heavily on purchased forecasts of the trends in their industry. Those making this type of investment in the service sector were all financial-

Table 6.2
The Use of Forecasting Techniques by Managers

Does your company develop in-house forecasts of demand?

Type of Company	Yes	No
Manufacturing (40)	40	0
Service (15)	12	3
High Tech (15)	14	1

Does your company purchase industry forecasts?

Type of Company	Yes	No
Manufacturing (40)	38	2
Service (15)	4	11
High Tech (15)	0	15

related companies. My only explanation as to why there is a pau-
city of purchased forecasts by the new, high-tech companies is that
these forecasts are very expensive and possibly unrelated to bur-
geoning high-tech fields.

ACTION ITEMS

☞ Understand clearly how your company and your industry
are influenced by economic fluctuations. You may consider
using consultants to define this for you and explain it to all
concerned. If appropriate, you may consider establishing
closer ties with a trade association to learn about these relationships. In any event, understand both why sales fluctuate and which economic indicators predict these fluctuations most accurately.

☞ Rely on your own instincts and expertise to formulate your
own leading economic indicators.

☞ Do not lose track of the fact that any economic indicator
should be interpreted cautiously. Do not overreact to
minor fluctuations.

☞ Help others follow these guidelines by keeping them informed of your long-run vision of the company.

Operating a Business in a Cyclical Economy

CHAPTER 7
Life Cycles and
Business Cycles

Consistency is a paste jewel that only cheap men cherish.
William Allen White

Industry and company sales vary over the life of a product. There are important business decisions to consider over the life cycle, including when or if to introduce a new product, what advertising strategies to adopt, how much to obligate to research and development (R&D), and what capital equipment to purchase. The way managers respond over the life cycle has far reaching implications.

Life cycles and business cycles are alike in one important respect. They both are consistently variable. Customers' demands for products—goods and services—not only vary because of swings in general economic activity but also because of changes in tastes. As new products come on the market, customers change their purchasing habits. This continuous pattern is referred to as the product life cycle.

The product life cycle is not independent of the business cycle. Therefore, an understanding of when the business cycle might change is related to how to manage effectively over the life of a product.

71

DO WE ALL KNOW ABOUT PRODUCT LIFE CYCLES?

Product life cycles are studied by every undergraduate business student. But, it is also a concept which appears regularly in popular press articles about sales forecasting or marketing strategies.

The concept is rather simple. As you can see in the upper diagram in Figure 7.1, when a new product is introduced into the market, industry sales first increase slowly (Introduction) then more rapidly (Growth). Sales eventually begin to level off (Maturity), and eventually fall (Decline). In other words, the life of a product is cyclical.

The product life cycle is not a theory about the profitability of a new product. There is nothing in Figure 7.1 about how well a new product will be received, how long it will survive, or how successful any one company will be in the industry. All the product life cycle tells us is that industry sales of a product will vary over the product's life.

The lower diagram in Figure 7.1 shows what a hypothetical company's sales may look like over the life cycle. As I have drawn it, company sales follow the same pattern of increase and decrease as do industry sales. If this company were an innovator and one of the first to introduce the new product, its sales pattern would show a faster rate of growth than the industry's. A fast imitator would also enjoy an earlier growth in sales. A late entrant into this industry may have a pattern of slowly increasing sales, possibly never reaching the same level as the company illustrated.

As a rule of thumb, product life cycles shorten as competition in the industry increases. Keep in mind that there is competition in all industries, and that competition takes many forms—price, design, quality, serviceability, advertising, and the like. When companies compete by introducing new and improved products, or when new technologies lead to the faster development of new products, then life cycles shorten. For example, the life cycle of video display terminals (VDTs) was extremely short—about two years in length. VDTs, often known as dumb terminals, were rapidly supplanted by intelligent terminals and comparably priced personal computers. The VDT life cycle became compressed as technologies quickly improved. At the other extreme are products

Figure 7.1
Stages During the Product Life Cycle

Industry Sales ($)

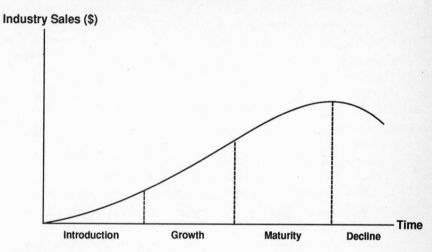

**A Representative
Company's Sales ($)**

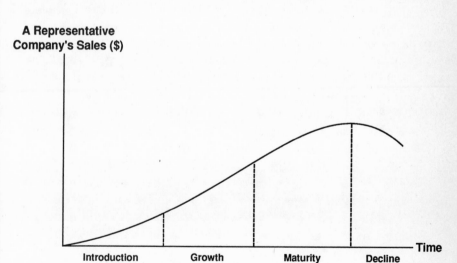

like scouring pads (e.g., SOS). This is a mature industry with few new product introductions. The life cycle is very long compared to the one in Figure 7.1.

Newspaper and magazine accounts of the competitiveness problems facing U.S. industries ask if life cycles are shortening. Of course they do not pose the question just that way. Rather, they editorialize that the U.S. has a competitive problem because technology-based products (like semiconductors or electronic products) are not being developed and marketed fast enough to keep pace with foreign competition. Most U.S. companies simply do not have the technology to keep pace.

How does the life cycle relate to the business cycle? Very simply. Swings in the business cycle affect the amplitude (height) and sometimes the length of a life cycle. When the economy is growing, industry sales (in most cases) are greater than when the economy is slowing down.

Figure 7.2 shows four life cycles, two for a product introduced and sold during an expansion, and two for a product introduced and sold during a contraction. Two things are clear from these diagrams. One is that the level of sales is considerably lower in the contraction than in the expansion. The other is that the life cycles are more compressed in an expansion than in a contraction.

It is difficult to generalize beyond the notions illustrated in Figure 7.2 as to how business cycles affect the length of life cycles. I am not being evasive. Such information depends upon many things, especially upon the competitive strategies used by firms in the industry and the purchasing habits of customers. Customers . . . this deserves *re-emphasizing*. It is useful for you to understand what happens over a business cycle and how to use economic indicators to anticipate better when cycles might occur. But this information is not a substitute for a firsthand understanding of your own customer base.

Returning to the point of how the business cycle affects the length of the product life cycle, consider two scenarios. In Scenario A, all indications are that the economy is in a period of prolonged growth. Most of the companies are competing with each other by introducing new or improved products. Foreign competitors are

Figure 7.2
Life Cycles in an Expansion and a Contraction

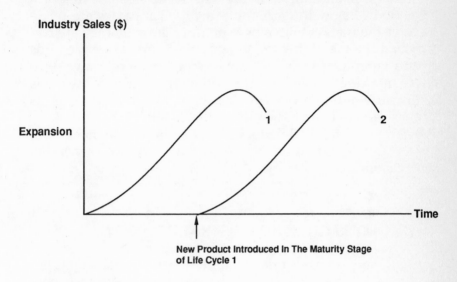

Industry Sales ($)

Expansion

1

2

Time

New Product Introduced In The Maturity Stage
of Life Cycle 1

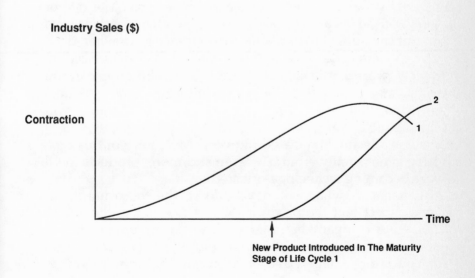

Industry Sales ($)

Contraction

2

1

Time

New Product Introduced In The Maturity
Stage of Life Cycle 1

also striving for a share of the U.S. market. As a result, life cycles are compact, as in the upper diagram in Figure 7.3.

In Scenario B, all indications are that the economy is in a prolonged period of slow to declining growth. Companies are reluctant to enter the market with a new product. Instead, they are trying to extend the life of their existing product until there are signs of renewed vigor. One company, however, takes an offensive position. They introduce a new product. Although the size of the pie is smaller because of the slowdown, this aggressive company expects to capture a larger share of the market that is left.

Whichever scenario describes an experience you have had, there is a logical question for you to ask: What do I do when the economy changes?

THE ECONOMY IS CHANGING—WHAT DO I DO?

There are no hard-and-fast rules to apply when an economy is entering an expansion or contraction. In Chapter 1, I explained how key economic variables move over the business cycle. The rate of inflation is cyclical, as are interest rates. Those are important facts to know, but they only begin to touch the surface as to when decisions have to be made. Let me emphasize that the choices faced by most managers are not black and white—do this in an expansion and do that in a contraction. Rather, an informed manager must perceive opportunities whenever they occur. Opportunities will vary over the life cycle.

Consider a technology-based industry. My choice of this type of industry is not totally arbitrary. More and more, products in all sectors are becoming technology-oriented.

As a manager, what would you do in the following situations? You expect that the product life cycle looks like the one in Figure 7.4. Your company has a good idea of its customers' tastes, and has a good track record of anticipating what the competition will do. You are at point A and your scheduling calls for you to introduce a new product in 12 months. Your guess is that your competitors will do the same thing.

Figure 7.3
Life Cycles in Two Hypothetical Situations

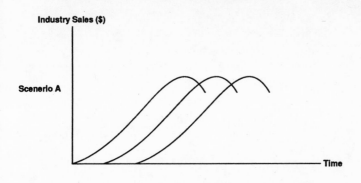

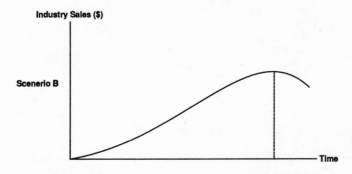

Figure 7.4
Life Cycles for a Technology-Based Industry

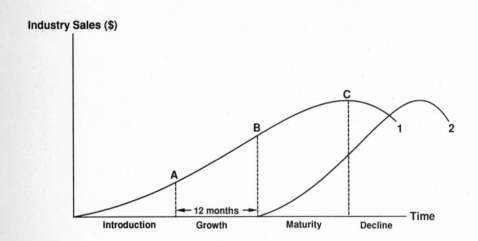

Situation A: You are at point A, 12 months prior to the scheduled introduction of the new product. New leading economic indicators point toward a weakening economy. Based on your own knowledge of your customers, you expect sales to soften within three months from now. In other words, you know that your industry will closely follow the economy.

You have no idea how long the slowdown will last. What will you do in this situation? Will you postpone introducing your new product? Will you cut back or increase the advertising efforts for your existing product?

You can predict certain industrywide effects:

- Life cycle 1 will shift down (lower industry sales over time) reflecting decreasing demand. It may also lengthen as customers postpone their purchases.

- Less profitable companies may postpone or cancel the introduction of their new products.

- Life cycle 2, representing the next generation of the product, may or may not shift down. This depends on the length of the recession. If it is short lived, the economy may be in a recovery period 12 months from now.

- Companies will likely increase their advertising in an effort to extend the maturity phase of life cycle 1. This is a hedge against the possibility of a prolonged recession. Advertising is frequently an effective anti-recession strategy, especially by companies trying to defend their market share.

What would you do in the situation just described? The answer to that question depends on how you and your planning staff respond to the following:

- Do we plan to change the introduction of our new product? What will our major competitor(s) do? If we speed up production, we may gain market share, especially if our customers are buying in anticipation of a short recession. If we enter the market late, we reduce the risk of exposing our product to our competitors and the possibility of having a financial loss.

- How do we divide our advertising budget between our current product and the new one? Should we focus our advertising on the new product? Are some advertising techniques more effective in good times than in bad?

- What about life cycle 3 (not shown, but it will follow life cycle 2)? Should we curtail our current R&D spending? If we do, what kind of competitive position will we be in three or four years down the road?

- Should we cut back on production workers during this slowdown? If it is short lived, will we have really saved money once we retrain new workers?

No one can answer these question with certainty, and there are no hard-and-fast rules of thumb for all managers to follow. Probably the best single answer is that *it depends*. Caution and an understanding that managing is not a mechanical science are good lessons to learn. Being aware that these are the types of questions to consider when the economy has its ups and downs is a first step toward perceiving new opportunities in an uncertain climate. Often, knowing the right questions to ask is a big step in the right direction.

Situation B: We are at point B. Everyone's new product has just been introduced. An economic slowdown is anticipated in about three months. From the industry's perspective it is a good guess that life cycle 1 will flatten out as demand slackens and companies try to extend the maturity stage.

The growth stage of life cycle 2 is directly affected by what the economy does. Some companies may have to close due do a lackluster response to their product.

At the company level, similar questions as in Situation A must be considered. The most important question concerns the division of resources between extending the sales of the existing product and pushing hard for sales of the just-introduced product. A reasonable case could be made to go ahead and introduce the new product, but not to push it very hard until the economy turns around. But a good case could also be made for going full steam ahead with the new product so as to gain a solid position in the market.

There are significant production costs associated with any new product. I have seen many companies postpone needed production changes, and even cut their R&D budgets, in situations like this in order to save money. In the short run, they are able to accomplish just that. But nine times out of ten, they regretted that decision down the road when their competitors were primed with a new product.

Situation C: We are at point C where industry sales of the existing product are beginning to decline—life cycle 1, and where industry sales of the new product introduced at point B, are just beginning to grow—life cycle 2. What if you now learn that the business cycle is expected to turn down in about 3 months?

This case is very similar to Situation A. There is nothing you or any manager can do to postpone the inevitable decline in life cycle 1. The pending slowdown may hasten it, but you would have been planning around a decline of one type or another. However, the expected slowdown may affect the introduction and product development strategy of some companies.

Demand probably will not slacken until life cycle 2 begins the growth stage. Keep in mind that this is a critical stage. When sales slow in the growth stage of the life cycle, revenues come in below expectation. This is problematic because important capital equipment investments are made at this point. (I will discuss this in more detail in the next section.) Also, this is the point in a product's evolution when a dominant product design emerges and when market shares are most vulnerable.

Revenues from the successful introduction of a new product are critical for funding the R&D needed for future products. Too often, R&D budgets are the first to go. Think about it. Without new products, what might the future look like? There may not be a life cycle 3 or 4 to worry about.

I expect that most companies would go ahead and introduce their product in this type of economic situation. But, the recession and associated shortfall in profit might cause some managers to become gun shy when it comes to financing their advertising campaign and the needed capital improvements. Think carefully about the long-run consequences of cutting back now on expenditures which are important to the long-run success of your business.

One of the many reasons offered for the competitiveness problems facing U.S. companies centers around too many short-sighted decisions. These involve making investment decisions to maximize *current* profit and earnings—which does keep the stockholders happy—rather than looking toward the *future*.

HAVE YOU HEARD OF THE PRODUCTION PROCESS LIFE CYCLE?

Production process life cycle is an academic buzz word. A production process life cycle is a teaching concept used in advanced business curricula. This fact aside, it is still a useful device for our purposes. It illustrates well some important business decisions which need to be made over the life cycle. And, as we just saw, these decisions can frequently become skewed when the business cycle is about to turn.

The production process life cycle and the product life cycle are closely related concepts. Whereas the product life cycle shows the growth and decline in industry sales, the production process life cycle relates such sales movements to important production decisions. See Figure 7.5.

Product characteristics change in response to consumer wants during the fluid stage of the production process life cycle. Production processes are changing too. They are labor intensive and are quite inefficient because generic purpose equipment is in place. Production runs are short.

In the transition stage, a dominant product design emerges. Remember Beta formatted videotapes? Does your computer use a DOS operating system? Once a dominant product design emerges, the production process begins to standardize. New, specialized equipment is used and average cost falls. Couple sales growth with falling average cost and profit will definitely increase.

In the specific stage the product has become standardized. Production becomes capital equipment intensive. Runs are long and only minor process changes are made. All of these characteristics are summarized in Table 7.1

The lesson to learn from this discussion is that there are important production decisions to be made over a product's life. These decisions directly affect the average cost of production and thus business profit. When the business cycle turns unexpectedly down, for instance, and when sales falter, investments in production technology become critically important. If, for example, a company did not make the necessary equipment decisions in the transition stage, even when total sales were down, it would not be positioned to compete cost effectively in the future. While a short-run labor-intensive process may save money now, it will cause the firm to lose money in the future.

Knowing these stages and the product/process characteristics in each is also important for suppliers. Suppliers are themselves

Figure 7.5
Comparing the Stages of a Product Life Cycle and a Production Process Life Cycle

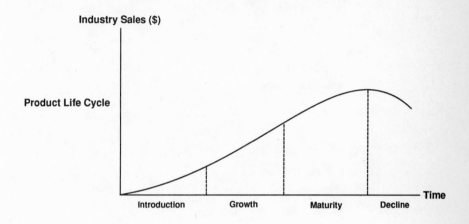

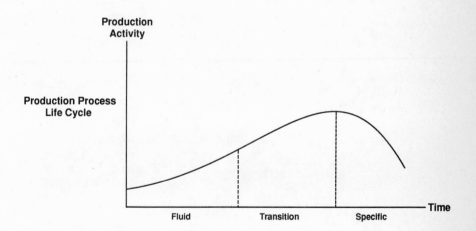

Table 7.1
Product and Process Characteristics over the Production Process Life Cycle

Stage	Product Characteristics	Process Characteristics
Fluid	Characteristics change frequently in response to consumer wants	—Production process is flexible —Labor intensive —Inefficient production —Use general purpose equipment —Short runs
Transition	Dominant product design emerges	—Specialized process —Purchase new capital
Specific	Standardized product	—Minor process changes —Capital intensive —Long runs

producers, and like you must anticipate cyclical swings and must know their customer base. They must anticipate how their customers will react in terms of equipment needs over the cycle and production process life cycle. In turn, their suppliers must do the same, and so on down the line.

RETAIL LIFE CYCLES

A retail life cycle is a somewhat ill-defined idea. It relates to the periodic introduction of retailing innovations. For example, according to NBER researchers there have been five major retailing innovations over the past 100 or so years: the downtown department store introduced in 1860, the variety store in 1910, the supermarket in 1930, the discount department store in 1950, and the home improvement center in 1965.

The retail life cycle concept comes into play in the following way. When a new retailing institution is introduced, it grows, matures, and declines just like any product innovation. However, not all retailing innovations have to be as major as the ones listed above to still be important and profitable. This then raises the important question as to the best time for a business to be innovative and introduce a retailing innovation.

Cost-plus retailing is one such innovation introduced in the late 1970s. Another was the gourmet grocery store with its classical music, complementary coffee, imported jelly beans, and the like. When is the best time to invest in such retail innovations?

In an expansion, customers are in the buying mood and such innovation may not be needed. But then again, an expansion may be the best time to develop customer loyalty. During a recession, especially if it is prolonged, it may be difficult for a business to absorb the costs of a new venture. As before, there is no right or wrong rule, but there is a series of questions which must be contemplated carefully. The better informed about potential cyclical movements in the economy, the better forewarned about these issues.

THE MANAGER'S VIEWPOINT

I asked the presidents/CEOs in the manufacturing sector how far in advance their company plans for the introduction of a new product. Of the 40 surveyed, 34 said that it was at least five years. Because of the lead time needed to compete successfully, it is imperative that long-run planning continuously take place *and* that long-run financial commitments remain firm to implement this planning. See Table 7.2.

I also asked this same question of the presidents/CEOs of the newly formed high-tech companies in my sample. They too plan ahead, but not quite as far ahead. Perhaps the life cycle of their industry is getting shorter due to the evolving nature of their products and to growing international competition.

Table 7.2
How Far In Advance Do Companies Plan?

How far in advance does your company plan for the introduction of a new product?

Type of Company	1 Year	3 Years	5 or More Years
Manufacturing (40)	0	6	34
High Tech (15)	0	14	1

ACTION ITEMS

☞ Think ahead. Today's product will not be marketable forever. Be prepared with new innovative products; be assured that your competitors will be doing this too.

☞ Act on new opportunities. Action may mean making a long-term investment: really good ideas do not occur every day.

☞ Do not fear long-term investments. Although the pay-back may be down the road, the cost of not keeping a stream of new innovative products in the pipeline may be even more costly.

☞ The more you know about the business cycle the better able you will be to anticipate when the market may be receptive to a new product.

CHAPTER 8

Profits and the Business Cycle

Thrift may be the handmaid and nurse of Enterprise. But equally she may not. . . . For the engine which drives Enterprise is not thrift, but Profit.

John Maynard Keynes

Profits are a leading indicator of economic activity and are an important consideration for business planning. In addition to being cyclical, fluctuations in profit are influenced by management's ability to operate a company efficiently.

Profit is important for at least four reasons.

- Profit, or more precisely the anticipation of profit, provides an incentive to managers to take risk, especially those who are compensated with bonuses or stock options.

- Movements in profit determine a company's dividend policy. Dividends are one reason people initially invest in a company.

- Movements in profit are carefully watched by stockholders. Falling profit often translates into a lower price per share, a possible cut in dividends, a possible takeover by

another company, and a general level of stockholder dis-
satisfaction.

- Movements in profit are an important consideration when
  raising equity capital or when considering the purchase of
  new capital equipment.

People watch profit levels very carefully. They make important decisions based on fluctuations in these levels. Owners invest
in their company primarily because of its profit potential. Because
profit moves up and down throughout the business cycle, it is important for both managers and investors to understand the difference between cyclical movements in profit and long-run profit
trends. The former are inevitable and the latter are determined by
competition and by the expertise—or lack of it—of management to
deal with the competition.

WHAT IS PROFIT?

Two definitions are important to the understanding of published
statistics on aggregate profit levels or balance sheet information
related to one company's profit. Before discussing these definitions, a broader view of profit should be mentioned, especially for
the entrepreneurially-minded reader.

Think of profit as the financial reward to the company for efficient management. This definition obviously departs from the traditional accounting approach to profit: revenue less cost. But when
you think about it, this definition makes a lot of sense.

Profit is revenue less cost. But what does a rising or falling
level of profit really reflect? How should such trends be interpreted? When revenue minus cost is positive it means the market values the company's product. Higher than average profit is attribut-
able to, among other things:

- a manager's ability to perceive accurately what customers
  want
- a manager's ability to produce his product at the lowest
  possible price while still maintaining quality

- a manager's ability to compete successfully in the market-place, that is, to rival the competition.

Regarding definitions, *aggregate* economic profit, Π, is:

$$\Pi = GNP - IBT - D - wL - R$$

where GNP is gross national product, IBT is indirect business taxes, D is depreciation, wL is the total wage bill (average wage, w, times total labor-hours, L), and R is interest paid by businesses. Thinking of GNP as the dollar value of all goods and services sold in a given year, then Π can be viewed as total aggregate revenue less all costs to produce those goods and services.

Company profit is similarly calculated. Starting with total sales revenue, subtract all relevant costs:

      Sales Revenue
−   <u>Returns and Allowances</u>
      Net Sales Revenue

−   Indirect Business Taxes
−   Depreciation
−   Payroll
−   Interest Expenses
−   <u>Cost of Goods Sold</u>
      After Tax Profit

DO PROFITS MOVE OVER THE BUSINESS CYCLE?

Aggregate profit, as well as any one company's profit, fluctuates quite a bit. It is critical to remember that these fluctuations are not necessarily abnormal. They are generally caused for two reasons. One is due to the inherent cyclical nature of the economy, and I will discuss that reason in this section. The other is that profit fluctuations relate directly to changes in managerial expertise. I will discuss this issue in the following section.

Movements in profit lead the business cycle. Profit turns down before the economy slows down, and profit turns up before an economywide recession is over. This leading pattern is shown by the index in Figure 8.1.

The aggregate profitability index is illustrated in Figure 8.2. This index is one of many indices calculated by the government, as published in *Business Conditions Digest*. This index, however, it is not part of the official composite index of leading economic indicators. The profitability index is calculated from three series: a stock price series, a corporate after tax profit series, and a price-to-unit cost series. As in Figure 8.1, note the cyclical pattern.

As the numbers along the profitability graph in Figure 8.1 indicate, aggregate profitability leads downturns in the business cycle by a year or so—note the exception of the two close recessions in the early 1980s—and it leads upturns in the business cycle by only a few months.

The government's after tax corporate profit series in Figure 8.2 also has a cyclical nature. It leads the business cycle, but does so by fewer months than the composite aggregate index in Figure 8.1.

The cyclical nature of profit is easy to explain by referring to the profit formulae explained above. Toward the end of an expansion sales level off, but interest rates and wages generally keep rising. These latter two prices—the price of borrowing and the price of labor—put a burden on companies to raise their prices in order to protect their profit levels. But with higher prices there is a decrease in demand. Higher prices, and the expectation of even higher prices, push wages and interest rates up even more. The end result is that profit falls.

As the economy turns down, sales decline. This decline puts even more downward pressure on profits. The decline will eventually soften as interest rates fall and less labor is employed. This result will, however, take time to develop.

Following a word of caution: do not think that when one company's profit falls it necessarily signals an economic slowdown is imminent. The fall in one company's profit may be nothing more than a market signal that their product is no longer in demand, or it may be that management is inefficiently operating the company.

Figure 8.1
Profit over the Business Cycle

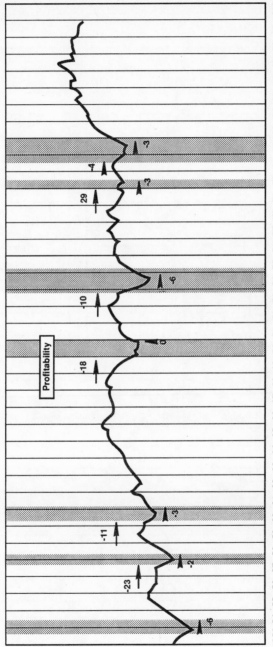

Source: *Business Conditions Digest.*

Figure 8.2
The Government's Profitability Index over the Business Cycle

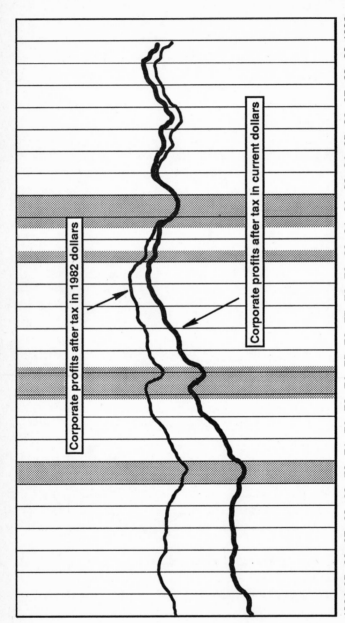

Corporate profits after tax in 1982 dollars

Corporate profits after tax in current dollars

1964 65 66 67 68 69 70 71 72 73 74 75 76 77 78 79 80 81 82 83 84 85 86 87 88 89 1990

Source: *Business Conditions Digest.*

Not all industries follow this same cyclical pattern with regard to their average profits. Certain industries are more recession proof than others. These are the so-called defensive industries. They offer products or services that customers purchase over the entire cycle. Thus, the profit levels of companies in these industries are, on average, more stable. Retail groceries, entertainment, tobacco products, selected textile products, proprietary drugs, and the like do not experience the same swings in sales over the cycle as do companies producing products in other industries. While companies in these defensive industries face the same profit-affecting problems as other companies—higher wages and interest rates—they are often in a better position to pass increased costs along to their consumers in the form of higher prices.

PERKS AND PROFIT

Not only will a company's profit go up and down over the business cycle, but also it will fluctuate depending on the diligence and expertise of its management. Some managers are better at their job than others. More efficiently run companies are generally those that are both more timely and creative in bringing new products to the marketplace and more innovative in ways to reduce their costs. It is not surprising to see in the annual editions of *Business Week* and *Fortune,* variability in profit levels between companies in the same industry.

Companies are owned by stockholders, and managers are ultimately responsible to these owners. However, most stockholders are not in a position to monitor how well management is doing to protect their investment interests. Boards of directors are not elected on the per se merits of their management skills. They are elected and re-elected on the basis of how closely the company's *actual* performance parallels the stockholders' *anticipated* performance.

Knowing the inability of stockholders to monitor the activities of management, it makes sense that managers will act in ways which will also benefit themselves. This does not mean that managers will ignore profit completely, but it does mean that managers may not act in a manner that maximizes the company's profit. Managers, just like each one of us, will pursue their own self-interest.

Managers satisfice. This term means that they will operate in a way that not only satisfies stockholders but also benefits themselves. Company jets, elaborate office suites, and Hawaiian conferences are not all that unpleasant. These perquisites, or perks, are possible, in part, because there is a lack of perfect information between owners and managers.

There is a one-to-one relationship between perks and profit. When perks go up, current profit goes down. I am not suggesting that *all* of management's perks are unnecessary. On the contrary, sometimes corporate jets are a valuable investment both for transportation and as a way to impress potential customers. And often, access to such amenities may be necessary for being able to hire the particular managers you want. I am suggesting that many companies have not reached their full profit potential, or perhaps have even failed, because of being overly extravagant or permitting their managers to pay more attention to fabric selection than to economic trends. There are some remedies, however.

More and more we see managers and key employees *at all levels* being paid salaries which have a component directly tied to the profit performance of the company. Stock options are one of the more frequently used incentives for managers to perform in a way which coincides with the financial interests of stockholders. In fact, at PepsiCo all 100,000 employees now receive annual stock options equal to 10% of their compensation. This trend is growing in both the manufacturing and service sectors. The studies I have seen or done comparing the overall performance of companies where top management has and does not have an equity stake strongly suggest that ownership provides an effective incentive for managers to operate in ways which increase corporate wealth. While tying managers' salaries to company performance will help to insure that all of their energies are devoted to protecting stockholders' investments, it will not fully indemnify the company from natural profit fluctuations. Business cycles are going to occur.

THE MANAGER'S VIEWPOINT

Some professional economists are now contending that the role of profit in the economy has diminished in recent years. Profit is still a leading indicator but, according to these analysts, the economy is becoming less dependent on profit for its fuel. In fact, such a viewpoint has recently earned the front page of *The Wall Street Journal*.

However, only 2 of the 40 manufacturing presidents/CEOs that I surveyed hold this view. Likewise, only 2 of those executives in the service sector and in high-tech companies concur. See Table 8.1. Maybe it is true that our economy is becoming less dependent on the fueling power of corporate profits, but I was hard pressed to find many top executives that believe this to be the case.

Table 8.1
The Role of Profit in the Economy

Do you believe that the importance of profit in fueling economic growth has decreased in recent years?

Type of Company	Yes	No
Manufacturing (40)	2	38
Service (15)	1	14
High Tech (15)	1	14

ACTION ITEMS

☞ Know why your company's profit fluctuates over time. Do not confuse quarterly fluctuations with long-term trends, either for your company or for the economy as a whole.

☞ Keep an open mind about changes in the demand for your product. Be objective about separating industrywide trends from company-specific trends. To do this you may have to listen objectively to what your marketing staff has to say. You may have to incorporate their ideas into your long-range plans in order to remain competitive. Do not lose sight of the fact that there are probably many perceptive individuals throughout your company.

☞ Learn about your cost structure and understand what specific elements are most susceptible to change when the economy changes. This exercise will take some time, but it will help you better determine how and why your profit fluctuates over the business cycle.

☞ Protect against satisficing behavior. Whenever possible tie manager/employee compensation to company performance.

CHAPTER 9
Pricing Strategies and the Business Cycle

Wisdom . . . teaches us to extend a simple maxim univer-
sally known. And this is, not to buy at too dear a price.

Henry Fielding

Companies use different pricing strategies. The effectiveness of
any one strategy varies over the business cycle and is directly related to the responsiveness of customers to price changes.

Managers do not set prices arbitrarily. Generally, producers of
a new or unique product initially use trial and error or experience
to determine the price the market will bear. But for the most part,
managers use a more systematic type of strategy to set prices. Regardless of the type of strategy used, the ultimate goal is to increase profit.

There are three fundamental concepts to remember when setting prices: customers have alternatives, customers respond to
price changes, and the effectiveness of any one pricing strategy
changes over the business cycle.

HOW DO YOUR CUSTOMERS REACT WHEN YOU CHANGE YOUR PRICE?

There is a term used by economists and marketers which is fundamental to this discussion. That term is *elasticity of demand.*

The word *elasticity* means responsiveness. A rubber band is
elastic; it responds when pulled upon. Customers (meaning both
consumers as well as other companies) respond in terms of their
purchases when prices change. What is imperative for you to
know is just how responsive your customers are to a price change.
Recall that I have emphasized throughout this book the importance of knowing your customer base. The more you know about
your customers, the better prepared you will be to make needed
changes over the business cycle.

You know that if you increase your price, the quantity demanded by your customers will decrease—this is the Law of Demand. The reason for this predictable inverse relationship is that
customers respond to the higher price in one of two ways: they
either find a substitute for your product and buy it, or they reduce
the amount of your product they buy (or they do both). If everyone in your industry increased their price, then customers could
not find lower priced substitutes. (I am *not* recommending price
collusion!) But, the total quantity sold in your industry would decrease as customers cut back on their total purchases.

Some examples will illustrate the managerial importance of
knowing how customers respond to a price change. Take some extreme cases.

Would you raise your price 50% if your knew with certainty
that your quantity sold would decrease by only 1%. You bet you
would! A 50% price increase would more than offset 1% fewer
items sold. Revenue would definitely increase, and profit would
likely do the same. Likewise, you would not reduce your price by
50% if you knew with certainty that your quantity sold would increase by only 1%. You would lower your price by 1% if you knew
with certainty that your quantity demanded would increase by
50%.

It is not a coincidence that retail stores put the same type of
items on sale season after season. They are the ones to which

customers will respond the most. A 20% off sale, say, will likely generate more than a 20% increase in quantity demanded. Retail stores want to make money even during a sale . . . and they generally do.

Some useful terminology related to customers' responses to price changes is defined in Exhibit 9.1. Pay particular attention to the adjectives *inelastic*—meaning relatively unresponsive—and *elastic*—meaning relatively responsive. It is easy to think of examples of an elastic and inelastic demand for goods and services. The demand for services offered by tax preparers is inelastic, meaning that most individuals are relatively unresponsive to a price change. In contrast, the demand for lawn care services is relatively elastic. Milk has an inelastic demand. Few people that I know stock up on milk or cut it out of their diets when the price changes. Do you often see milk on sale? In comparison, the demand for televisions is fairly elastic—consumers are very responsive to a price change.

CYCLES AND PRICE RESPONSES

Customers respond differently to price changes at various times over the business cycle. As I have summarized in Exhibit 9.2, customers pay more attention to price changes in a contraction than in an expansion. If demand is elastic, it is even more so in a contraction than in an expansion. If demand is inelastic, it is even more so in an expansion than in a contraction.

The following guidelines may be useful to you in thinking about your own pricing strategy. Like all generalities, they apply to some industries' products more so than to others. In a contraction, as you know, customers budget more carefully than in an expansion. Consumers budget more carefully in anticipation of less income. Income can decrease because of unemployment or because of lower investment yields due to the lower interest rates. Companies act in the same way. They budget more carefully in a contraction in response to lower profit. In an expansion, customers are relatively less responsive to price changes. Consumer income

Exhibit 9.1
Terminology on Customers' Responses to Price Changes

Example

> Price increases 10% and quantity demanded decreases 8%, or
> Price decreases 10% and quantity demanded increases 8%

> Customers are relatively unresponsive and demand is said to be <u>inelastic</u>.

Generalization

> If the percentage change in price is greater than the percentage change in quantity demanded by customers, then demand is <u>inelastic</u>.

Example

> Price increases 8% and quantity demanded decreases 10%, or
> Price decreases 8% and quantity demanded increases 10%

> Customers are relatively responsive and demand is said to be <u>elastic</u>.

Generalization

> If the percentage change in price is less than the percentage change in quantity demand by customers, then demand is <u>elastic</u>.

Predictable Relationships

> If price increases and demand is <u>elastic</u> then revenue will decrease.
> If price decreases and demand is <u>elastic</u> then revenue will increase.
> If price increases and demand is <u>inelastic</u> then revenue will increase.
> If price decreases and demand is <u>inelastic</u> then revenue will decrease.

Exhibit 9.2
Customer Responses to Price Changes over the
Business Cycle

IN A CONTRACTION, the following key economic variables generally decrease:

    interest rates
    inflation
    employment levels
    real income
    real after tax profit.

    Therefore customers become more responsive to price changes (demand becomes more elastic).

IN AN EXPANSION, the following key economic variables generally increase:

    interest rates
    inflation
    employment levels
    real income
    real after tax profit.

    Therefore customers become less responsive to price changes (demand becomes more inelastic).

and company profit increase and overall confidence about the future is higher than in a contraction.

Regarding pricing strategies, a price decrease may be relatively more effective in a contraction than in an expansion. Likewise, the ability to pass cost increases along to customers is greater in an expansion than in a contraction. I realize this prescription sounds like common sense (and it is), but in my experience with companies when they formulate their pricing strategies, even the simplest guidelines are overlooked until it is too late to do something. Too often I see managers trying to devise elaborate pricing structures presumably to outwit both the competition and the customer. I wonder more times than not if these individuals are really trying to outwit their VPs in hopes of a promotion. My advice to you and to every manager, at every level, is not to overlook the obvious.

ALTERNATIVE PRICING STRATEGIES

For a new business, or an existing one trying to introduce a new product, the best rule of thumb is to price initially with the competition, and then see what happens. I know this is not a very sophisticated strategy, but there is really no efficient way for you or any manager to know what price the market will bear until the market has been tested. If *you* have not tested it, then rely on what experience you see that others have. A word of caution, however. Do not become wedded to the first price you try. Managers often err in their perception of what their customers will buy, what level of quality they perceive, and how much they will ultimately pay. Your marketing group must be aware of the need for a price change, and it must have management's support so it can respond. This is true in all sized companies. One way for your marketing group to sharpen their perceptive powers is for them to become more familiar with the customer either through marketing survey information or field-based experience with sales people.

My favorite classroom example of how to build a marketing group that is not perceptive of change comes from a regional tobacco manufacturer whose policy it is never to promote anyone from their sales department into marketing. The marketing vice president once told me that he only hires new graduates so that he can train "their uncluttered minds." Would it be so terrible if their minds were partially filled with some real world sales experience about the company's product?

For the more established company, experience often provides the best benchmark. I never cease to be amazed at how well managers who know their customer base can anticipate fairly precisely their customers' reaction to a price change. This is not to say that some fine tuning may not be in order from time to time.

The two most prevalent pricing strategies in private sector companies and in some service companies are cost-plus (mark-up) pricing and price discrimination. Neither follows any hard and fast rule. Both need to be customized to take into account the economy's ups and downs.

Cost-Plus Pricing

The basic concept here is to set your price at a level which covers your average cost of production. Then, add to this price an additional amount for profit. You could call this additional amount— the plus part of cost-plus pricing—the profit factor.

Many enterprises price this way. Contractors often bid for jobs on a cost-plus basis, say cost of materials and labor plus 15%. The 15% covers their indirect costs, such as insurance, as well as their profit margin. Discount furniture stores sell name brand furniture at some percentage off of the retail list price. If the list price of furniture is twice the cost, then this pricing scheme is nothing more than a variant of a cost-plus strategy. Consulting companies follow the same strategy. They bid on contracts at direct cost plus an overhead percentage (which covers the rent and the perks), plus a profit factor. Even retail grocery stores price, on average, at a fixed profit mark-up of about two to three percent over cost.

For those managers who use such a pricing strategy, some care and thought must go into determining the optimal size of the profit factor at different times over the business cycle. The final price must be competitive. If it is too high, customers will eventually shift their business to others. If it is too low, then business will increase but some potential profit will have been lost.

Of course, there are justifiable reasons for one company, like yours perhaps, to price higher than the competition if their product is worth more. Customers will pay a premium for higher quality, better pre-sale and after-the-sale service, and other such amenities. Whether to offer such attributes in a product is an important marketing consideration, but make sure the customer knows they are getting these extras. Customers will not pay for something they do not know they are getting.

There are times when your price may equal your competitors',
but your profit factor may be greater because your average cost is
lower. This is a very desirable position to be in. It occurs when a
company makes cost saving investments, such as initiating a new
organizational structure or utilizing a more efficient piece of
equipment that is not duplicated by competitors.

Regarding the size of the profit factor and the business cycle,
managers might consider varying their cost-plus formula to account for possible economic fluctuations. If customers are naturally relatively unresponsive to price changes, then they are even
more unresponsive during an expansion than during a contraction.
Therefore, cost increases can more easily be passed along to these
customers in an expansion than in a contraction. If customers are
naturally relatively responsive to price changes, then they are even
more responsive in a contraction than in an expansion. When the
economy slows, try hard to avoid passing cost increases along to
your customers. In general, they are overly sensitive to price increases and may react in a way so as to lower profit more than if
the cost increases were internalized. You may even lose them for
good. An expansion, and they always follow a contraction, is the
better time to recover from previous profit losses.

Price Discrimination

The term *discrimination* generally has a negative connotation. The
term often refers to biased treatment toward a group based on
their race, age, or sex. With regard to pricing, the term *discrimination* is used to refer to different prices being changed to different
groups of customers. Such a pricing strategy is widely practiced
and is often profitable. Like a cost-plus strategy, the effectiveness
of price discrimination varies over the cycle.

The two elements needed for price discrimination are separate
markets so that there can be no resale of the product, and separate
groups of customers, each with a different degree of price responsiveness. Some everyday examples of price discrimination are children, adult, and senior citizen movie ticket prices. Senior citizens
and the parents of children are more responsive to the price of a

movie ticket than are other viewers. A movie ticket cannot be re-sold to a person in another category (an adult cannot use a child's ticket). You always see the higher price charged to the adults. This type of pricing scheme comes under the heading of price discrimination.

Airlines also practice price discrimination. For a person to qualify for a super saver discount fare, they must usually spend a Saturday night on their trip. Generally, businesspeople travel on weekdays and have an expense account. Businesspeople, as a group, are less responsive to price changes than are vacationers. For most businesspeople, time is the more important factor. Vacationers can generally plan ahead to spend the Saturday night in order to receive the 50% or so discount.

In a contraction, it benefits a company to discriminate more than in an expansion. In a contraction, vacationers are even more responsive to the lower price. Parents are usually more sensitive to sending children to movies. Thus, price decreases will increase revenue more so in a contraction than in an expansion.

More and more companies are catering to senior citizen groups. Promotional pricing is used increasingly to attract the business of this growing segment of the economy. Price discrimination is a very logical pricing strategy for a company to adopt, especially in a contraction.

THE MANAGER'S VIEWPOINT

It is heartening to hear from senior executives that the guidelines I have suggested here are useful to them. While you will readily see in Table 9.1 that most of the interviewees already consider business cycle fluctuations when formulating their pricing strategy, two-thirds of those who have not done so in the past plan to begin to do so in the future.

Table 9.1
Managers and Their Pricing Strategies

Does your company modify its pricing strategy over the business cycle?

Type of Company	Yes	No
Manufacturing (40)	24	16
Service (15)	10	5
High Tech (15)	6	9

Having read this chapter, will you now begin to think about the business cycle when implementing your pricing strategy?

Type of Company	Yes	No
Manufacturing (40)	33	7
Service (15)	13	2
High Tech (15)	14	1

ACTION ITEMS

☞ Know your customers. Know why they want to buy your product and how responsive they are to price changes.

☞ Know your competitors' products. How substitutable is your product with others'?

☞ Keep abreast of industry trends for both price changes and the economywide rate of inflation. This information provides a useful benchmark if you need to increase your price.

☞ Keep your pricing strategies simple. Remember there are a lot of people in your own company who have to understand and implement them. If your customers are very sensitive to price changes, think about non-price strategies for increasing revenues.

CHAPTER 10
Labor Productivity and the Business Cycle

Measure not the work
Until the day's out and the labor's done.

Elizabeth Barrett Browning

All companies need to measure the productivity of their workers. An output per worker measure is applicable only when employees are doing routine, assembly-line like tasks. Output per worker is not well suited for comparing labor's productivity across units within a company or for comparing changes in productivity over time. Output per worker can fluctuate over time due to managers' errors in judgement about the business cycle. A total factor productivity measure is much better.

THE DO'S OF OUTPUT PER WORKER

The most common measure of labor productivity is output per worker, often represented as Q/L (Q represents output and L represents labor—number of workers or number of worker hours).

Such an index is very appealing. If worker productivity increases, then more units of output are produced per person or per hour. If a company has 10 workers who produce a total of 100 units per day, and the number of units increases to 110 per day, then it is clear that worker productivity increased: Q/L increased from 10 to 11. Could there be any other explanation?

This output per worker approach to measuring labor productivity is useful in two situations: one, where output is easily quantified, as in number of units per hour, and the other, where the capital equipment used by the workers is the same. Output per worker measures are frequently used within a company to evaluate the productivity of assembly lines, secretarial pools, data processing units, or any other collection of responsibilities which consists of repeatable activity. Even sports figures are ranked, and generally paid, in terms of hits at bat or yards per carry. Similarity of the task is the key element if you are going to use an output per worker measure to compare the productivity of workers.

When productivity is measured this way, the more astute managers will also evaluate and reward their workers based on this measure. As an aside, it is my experience that few things are worse for employee morale than to learn that salary adjustments are made only on the basis of subjective information when objective data are gathered and used by managers for other purposes.

Output per worker measures are also useful for comparisons of changes in aggregate economic activity. The Bureau of Labor Statistics calculates output per worker for all individuals employed in the private business sector, the private nonfarm sector, and the manufacturing sector. These estimates are published in data tables in their *Monthly Labor Review*. Such statistics are helpful for describing long-run trends in the economy.

As you can see from Table 10.1, labor productivity grew very slowly during the 1970s in all three of the economy's main sectors. It is not by coincidence that this was also the same time period during which the U.S. economy reached it lowest level of competitiveness in world markets.

Table 10.1
Compound Annual Rates of Growth in Output Per Worker

Sector	1948-87	1948-73	1973-79	1979-87
Private Business	2.3	2.9	0.6	1.4
Private Nonfarm	1.9	2.5	0.5	1.2
Manufacturing	2.7	2.8	1.4	3.3

Source: Bureau of Labor Statistics.

THE DON'TS OF OUTPUT PER WORKER

I do not ever recommend using output per worker:

- to compare the productivity of workers doing different jobs
- to compare the productivity of separate business units within a company
- to evaluate the productivity of either a business unit, or the company as a whole, over time.

In other words, output per worker measures are limited in their applicability. They should therefore be used very carefully. When used, they should be accompanied by other information. This rule can be generalized to reinforce what I have previously said about economic indicators. Never rely on just one.

The fact of the matter is that output per worker measures are widely used to quantify labor productivity and to compare it across business units and within a business unit at different points in time. Why? Convenience. Why do I never recommend using this measure? Simple; I am concerned about accuracy.

Output per worker, Q/L, is very easy to calculate and to report to others. The fact that it is often difficult to measure output precisely has not stopped many managers from going ahead and performing the necessary division. I am sympathetic with these individuals, especially those in middle management positions. I have been in that position myself. All too frequently, terse directives come down from above asking for information to document a unit's productivity gains for the year. All too frequently, middle managers know their unit's next budget will be based on the seemingly objective information they send back upstairs. It is so easy to fall back on a Q/L measure, whether it accurately describes reality or not.

The middle manager is in a dilemma not of his own making. Upper management should know better than to look for simple cross-unit comparisons. There is no single statistic which accurately captures the subtleties involved in making comparisons across individuals doing different jobs, or across business units with different objectives. This is true even when the Q and the L in the Q/L calculation are measured precisely!

As another aside, if upper management has chosen their middle managers correctly, then within-unit evaluations should continuously be taking place through dialogue and should never be reduced to a year-end number. Upper management should be meeting on a regular basis with middle managers to understand better how each unit is meeting its goals and objectives, and to help them reformulate them as corporate goals and objectives change. This is a time-consuming process and clearly one which does not reduce to a simple ratio of output to number of employees. Time consuming or not, in the long run it is effective and generally has a rather large payback.

Why is an output per worker measure so bad? Consider some commonly made errors.

When comparing across individuals or business units the implicit assumptions behind a Q/L index are that the output produced in one unit is equivalent to the output produced in another unit and that the units of labor are the same. Rarely is this the case.

Take the manufacturing and marketing units of a textile company. What does it mean for manufacturing to produce 10 bolts of fabric per person-hour and for marketing to produce $3,000 of new orders per salesperson. Which is the more productive unit? There is no way to tell.

Admittedly, my example is overly simplistic. However, when time is added as another dimension, the situation becomes more complicated and the use of a Q/L measure becomes even more prone to error. Within a business unit, output per worker will vary over the business cycle in ways which are totally unrelated to how efficiently workers work.

Consider points A, B, and C on the hypothetical business cycle in Figure 10.1. Recall that at any point in time there is some uncertainty as to where the economy will be in the future. I have obviously drawn this business cycle with perfect foresight about when the turning points will occur. Unfortunately, you will never have that luxury when making important decisions.

Figure 10.1
Measuring Labor Productivity over the Business Cycle

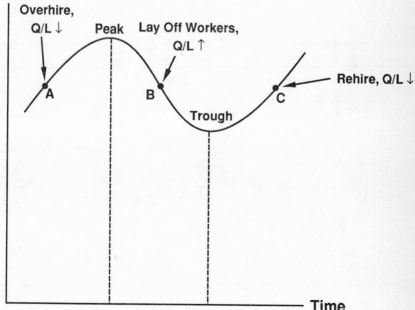

There is often a tendency on the part of managers to be overly optimistic about the length of an expansion. You may have experienced this, too? Even when faced with information about economic indicators, there is a natural feeling that the company's good times are "my own doing" and that they will continue. From my experience, these views are especially true for middle managers. They often sense that they are being evaluated for promotion based on their optimism and aggressiveness. As a result, it is not uncommon for business units under middle manager supervision to overhire in the latter stages of an expansion.

At point A in the figure, middle managers are likely to increase their work force in anticipation of continued growth in demand. If sales do not continue to grow at their previous pace and start to slow as the business cycle's peak is reached, then Q/L will decrease (because the denominator, L, is increasing faster than the numerator, Q). In other words, this unit's measured productivity will be falling as the business cycle, and presumably the company, peaks. The simple explanation for this curiosity is that this unit's manager was overly aggressive and tried to hire too many workers. The manager erred; the workers' true productivity may not have changed.

Note that I referred to measured productivity in the previous paragraph. From point A to the peak the actual productivity of continuing employees probably increased. As the new workers came on board, the Q/L index went down.

This same statistical phenomenon could occur if output is measured in terms of the dollar value of the unit's output. If this unit's sales had been increasing *only* because prices had been going up with inflation, then measured productivity may have been going up but actual productivity might have been falling. If there is overhiring, even an inflation-adjusted output per worker measure will go down.

There is also a tendency for middle managers to hold on to labor well into the downturn of a business cycle. This is not necessarily a bad management practice. Recruiting and training costs are not trivial. These costs can often be greater than the losses associated with retaining temporarily unneeded workers. And, downturns generally are shorter lived than expansions.

One general rule of thumb is that recruiting and training costs equal four to five times the annual salary of the replaced worker. These additional costs include not only the new individual's salary, but also the costs associated with the lost work time of those training the new worker and the time it takes for the new employee to come up to speed. Is it any wonder that companies today are exerting more effort to retain quality workers than ever before? When unemployment is low toward the peak of a business cycle, quality employees may not even be able to be found.

Therefore, at point B in Figure 10.1, when the necessary labor adjustments are finally made, Q/L might well increase if labor is reduced faster than output is falling. As a result, measured output per worker could be increasing as the business cycle tends into a recession, even if the actual productivity of the workers is unchanged.

Finally, with reference to point C, as the business cycle just begins to turn up there is a natural reluctancy to hire new workers to meet increased demand. Managers logically want to make sure the expansion is real. As a result, Q will be growing and so will Q/L. Once the new workers are hired, the unit's output per worker will likely fall. Falling worker productivity in the face of an expanding market might well be misunderstood by a less than thoughtful top executive.

Therefore, it is not at all uncommon for a unit's measured labor productivity to decrease in the latter stages of an expansion, to increase well into a recession, and then to fall when the company is expanding in the next recovery stage. This volatility can result solely from the hiring practices of middle managers and may not be related at all to the efficiency with which workers work. See Exhibit 10.1.

There are even more problems associated with a Q/L measure of labor productivity. Labor is not the only factor used by a company to produce its goods and services. Production depends on many inputs, including equipment and raw materials.

Take a situation where new equipment is introduced into a business unit. This might be some elements of a flexible manufacturing system within a manufacturing setting, a new electronic data processing unit in a financial center, or an electronic scanner

Exhibit 10.1
The Volatility of Q/L over the Business Cycle

With reference to point A in Figure 10.1, this hypothetical unit produced 20,000 parts per hour using 100 workers. Q/L is 200. Based on an expected growth in sales of 10%, 10 additional workers are hired. What actually materializes is a 5% increase in sales. Output increases from 20,000 to 21,000 parts per hour. With 110 workers, Q/L falls to 191—a 4.5% decline in measured productivity.

With reference to point B, the hypothetical unit is again producing 21,000 parts per hour using 110 workers. Sales are expected to fall so major cut-backs in employees are made. Production slips to 19,000 parts per hour with only 90 workers employed. Output per worker goes up from 191 to 211—a 10.5% increase in the midst of a forthcoming recession. That looks pretty good on paper.

At point C, output rebounds from 19,000 to 20,000 parts per hour. Labor also increases in anticipation of the expansion—from 100 to 110 workers. Q/L falls in this expansion from 190 to 182.

in a retail store. If the new equipment is used properly, output should increase and fewer workers should be needed. To no surprise, output per worker will increase, but not because the workers are more efficient. The productivity increases being attributed to labor from a Q/L measure really should be attributed to the equipment. Output per unit of capital equipment is what increased. A good case could be made that the salary rewards associated with such an increase in productivity should go to that individual who championed the idea to buy the new equipment, more so than to those who are using it.

The point is, Q/L is not independent of the efficiency with which equipment is used or introduced into the company.

A BETTER WAY—TOTAL FACTOR PRODUCTIVITY

In 1975, [Harold] Golle [Operations Vice President] asked Bill Brady [Manager of Industrial Engineering] and Ed McNesby [Manager of Cost Systems] to take on the task of designing . . . a productivity program for General Foods. . . . [They sought one] that focused on the most . . . competitive . . . elements . . . which suggested that a measure of "total factor productivity" would be more appropriate for GF's business than the usual simple measure of labor productivity.

                                                    HBS Case Services

Because there are many factors besides labor which influence production in a company, a productivity measure capturing the influence of all factors on output is more appropriate than one which only captures labor's influence. Total factor productivity, often abbreviated as TFP, measures the contribution of total inputs to output. It represents output per unit of all factors of production.

Conceptually, this approach to evaluating a business unit's overall productivity, or that of an entire company, makes a lot of sense. However, it is not calculated as easily as Q/L. It is $Q/($all inputs$)$. The denominator is somewhat complicated because all of the inputs used must be weighted in such a way that they can be combined. Accountants are well equipped to do this exercise. But then, the calculations are out of the direct control of the manager needing the data. There is a tradeoff to be made, but one I think you should be willing to make. Accuracy in the calculation of productivity is imperative if the data are to be used for either evaluation purposes or for setting a new corporate strategy.

WHAT IS PRODUCED IN THE SERVICE SECTOR?

Any time efforts are made to evaluate productivity, labor productivity in particular, the produced output must be quantifiable. This can be problematic in the service sector. How do you measure the output of a doctor, a lawyer, an accountant, or a teacher? Do you look at the number of patients seen in a given day? Does this measure take into account the quality of the doctor's examination? Does an accounting firm look only at the number of billable hours? No; quality, customer satisfaction, and client retention are equally important to these professionals.

This problem of measuring the productivity of service-oriented companies is not easily solved. It has long plagued managers as well as academic researchers. It is my experience from consulting with service companies that the more involved top managers are in the daily activities of such an enterprise, the more accurate is their intuition when a marginal dollar is allocated to the more productive unit. This is a good example of when a formula does not work well.

I am fully aware that there are many formula-based books on the market and equally as many seminar series for you to attend on how to measure productivity in the service sector. But I think that you should exercise caution before jumping on this band wagon. Although I am in favor of indexing performance—and I prefer a TFP measure to a Q/L measure—any measure must be based on a reliable quantification of output. Output, in my opinion, is extremely difficult to measure in the service sector, or the public sector for that matter. When I have been asked to formulate service sector company performance indices, they are complicated and they are never easily reduced to a simple ratio of accounting information. When I do develop such models, I also make it clear to the top managers for whom I am working that they should never forget their instinct may be just as accurate as my mathematics.

This conclusion is especially important given that business activities vary over the business cycle. Because of the ups and downs in the overall economic environment, special care must be made not to jump to the conclusion that slackening sales are due to a decrease in labor productivity, or that when sales fall new equipment is the only answer to boosting productivity and profit.

THE MANAGER'S VIEWPOINT

Of the 40 top executives from the manufacturing companies I interviewed, 39 reported to me that they regularly receive budget requests in which the productivity gain of the requesting unit is quantified by an output-per-worker ratio. I was not at all surprised that these same 39 executives overwhelming rejected the notion that *their* productivity, leadership, and overall contribution could be measured in the same way!

Table 10.2
A New Viewpoint on Output Per Worker

Do you regularly receive from your vice presidents budget requests that include output per worker calculations?

Type of Company	Yes	No
Manufacturing (40)	39	1

Do these requests assume that output per worker measures labor's productivity?

Type of Company	Yes	No
Manufacturing (40)	39	0

Would you like your performance judged on the basis of this same ratio?

Type of Company	Yes	No
Manufacturing (40)	0	39

ACTION ITEMS

☞ Systematically evaluate the productivity of all your workers. Reward them accordingly. Make the effort to look at more than one productivity measure.

☞ Develop productivity measures which will be relevant to you as well as to your subordinates.

☞ Make the effort to develop a TFP-like index to use for the entire company as well as for smaller groups.

☞ Learn how sensitive your productivity measures are to business cycle fluctuations. This will take some time, but hopefully you will retain your productivity measures for quite a few years.

CHAPTER 11
Inventories and the Business Cycle

Providence is always on the side of the last reserve.

Napoleon

Inventories are a lagging economic indicator. They reflect managers' misperceptions about fluctuations in demand. When valuing inventories, a replacement cost approach is recommended, but replacement costs move with the business cycle.

Perhaps history will chronicle just-in-time inventory management as one of the top ten buzz words for the 1980s. The popular press has certainly had a heyday with their generally uninformed views of Japanese management and, in particular, of just-in-time inventory control. As an aside I might add that the success of Japanese management has been due to, in my opinion, their ability to select and implement the best aspects of American management.

In this chapter I am not going to discuss the specifics of just-in-time inventory management, but rather discuss general aspects of inventory management which are directly related to the business cycle. Just-in-time is important—obtaining a constant flow of material parts so that no one supplier in the chain has inventories—but my guidelines are intended to be more general in nature rather than only for that practice.

INVENTORIES AND THE BUSINESS CYCLE

Inventories are a lagging economic indicator. Several inventory-related series are collected and have been reported in *Business Conditions Digest*. Being lagging indicators, these series do not gain the same degree of attention as do many of the leading indicators. This fact should not undermine the importance of inventories as an economic or corporate barometer. Unfortunately, we all probably get more caught up in wanting to know what the future holds rather than wanting to know where we have already been.

The diagram in Figure 11.1 shows five time series of inventory-related data from *Business Conditions Digest*. Each series lags the business cycles shown by the shaded recession years. What is particularly striking from these diagrams is how smoothly the inventory series move over time. They do not reflect the same volatility as prices or interest rates.

WHY DO INVENTORIES LAG THE BUSINESS CYCLE: ARE MANAGERS SLOW TO REACT?

No, managers are not slow to react to changes in the economy. The point is that any reaction must *follow* an event. Of course, you could make a good argument that managers should be anticipating cyclical swings and making inventory decisions based on those expectations. If this were the case, then inventories would move more closely with the cycle. The fact of the matter is that this very rarely happens. Too often inventories accumulate because a manager misjudged a downturn, or they accumulate when an upswing in the cycle was unanticipated. One of the consequences of Bill Lawrence's miscalculation of the slowdown in the economy was an inventory surplus of electronic parts.

From the schematic in Figure 11.2, you can easily see how interrelated inventory decisions are. The final sellers of a product base their inventories on the anticipated or actual demand of their

Figure 11.1
Inventories and the Business Cycle

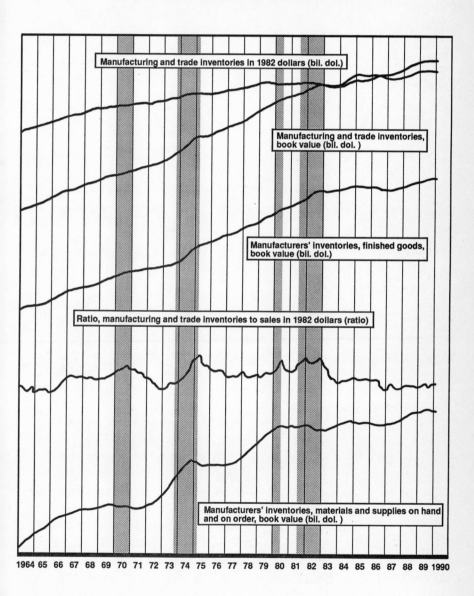

Manufacturing and trade inventories in 1982 dollars (bil. dol.)

Manufacturing and trade inventories, book value (bil. dol.)

Manufacturers' inventories, finished goods, book value (bil. dol.)

Ratio, manufacturing and trade inventories to sales in 1982 dollars (ratio)

Manufacturers' inventories, materials and supplies on hand and on order, book value (bil. dol.)

1964 65 66 67 68 69 70 71 72 73 74 75 76 77 78 79 80 81 82 83 84 85 86 87 88 89 1990

Source: *Business Conditions Digest.*

Figure 11.2
Inventories and the Customer-Supplier Relationship

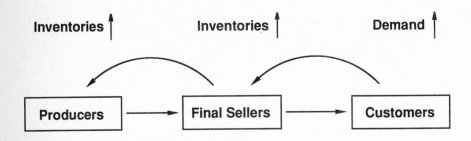

customers. The suppliers of intermediate products in turn base their inventory needs on the final sellers' demands, and so on. For complex final products, you can easily see how intricate this inventory decision process can become. One misjudgment can send ripples through the system.

The most critical inventory management decision generally comes at the point in time when a business cycle begins to turn up. According to noted author Hal Mather, "wrong decisions made at this point will affect not only the sustainability of the recovery but also a company's performance during and after the boom period." It is clear from the schematic in Figure 11.2 just how many companies can be affected by a misforecast demand. If each player in the integrated scheme of things accumulates inventories based on their customers' initial demand increase as the cycle turns up, and if either these demands are exaggerated or the economy has a false start, then there will be snowballing ramifications.

Although they will not admit this, even in confidential consulting relationships, I firmly believe managers at all levels overestimate the demand for their product when the cycle begins to turn up. Why is this the case? I can only speculate, but three reasons come to mind:

- During an economic slowdown, especially a prolonged one, suppliers often lose contact with their customers. As a result, they have less information to rely upon about their future demand needs.

- Also, during such periods, suppliers have a tendency to forget that their competitors may be using slack time to formulate new, aggressive strategies. As a result, when demand turns up there is a tendency to overstate the market share which might be received.

- A single increase in the demand for your product does not establish a long-run trend. It is difficult to forecast demand. It is even more difficult to forecast the timing of demand. Both are needed if inventories are to be managed efficiently.

Is it any wonder that production and sales managers have it in their vocabularies that "we need inventories now," "we need more capacity and lead time," and "we need more workers to prepare for future growth." Because expansions are generally longer lived than recessions, many think there is some safety in accumulating inventories. They will eventually be used. I disagree with this logic.

The key to effective inventory management is to be able to forecast accurately your customers' real long-run demand. You might react to this statement by thinking that my remark is trivially obvious. In a sense, it is an obvious statement. But, as I have stated previously, I have learned from both my consulting experience and from talking with others that this simple perception is all too often overlooked.

Suppose you are the manager of a company which supplies electrical components to a final producer of an electronic product. Your customer is placing some large orders for components.

(Maybe your customer is Bill Lawrence?) Is his demand real? Is his behavior a good barometer of what other customers will shortly do? Should you increase your inventory levels in response to his orders? The answer is yes, if you believe that the aggregate demand for this electronic product is strong *and* will be sustained so as to justify your inventory costs. But if you believe this customer has misjudged the market's strength, then the answer is no. You have to *perceive* beyond your immediate customer and gauge the probability that his demand is real and will last. Then, you have to *act. Perception* and *action* are key entrepreneurial traits. When present in an individual, their company will generally do very well.

HOW TO VALUE INVENTORIES OVER THE CYCLE

Valuing inventories is important when making the decision to engage in a business venture. The accepted accounting method for valuing inventories is to do it on the basis of acquisition cost. That is, the value of an inventory item is the cost that you paid to acquire it. However, from an economic perspective, inventories should be valued not at their acquisition cost, but rather at their replacement cost. The reason for this is that replacement cost best reflects the market's current value of the resource. Do you value employees on the basis of the salary they earned when first employed? I doubt it! You probably value them in terms of how the market values their productivity as reflected in products and in alternative job prospects. Because the replacement cost of most inventories varies with the cycle, so too does the value of these inventories.

Consider a simple example. You own a company which designs and installs data base management systems in small businesses. Your costs for a job include labor and equipment. You inventory all of the equipment normally needed to complete a job. You have the opportunity to take on a $50,000 job. Should you accept it? Three situations are described in Table 11.1.

In all of these cases, the labor costs for the job are $15,000. In the first situation, the inventoried equipment is valued at its acqui-

Table 11.1
Alternative Methods for Valuing Inventories

Categories	Case 1	Case 2	Case 3
	Cost of Equipment at Acquisition Cost	Cost of Equipment at Replacement Cost in an Expansion	Cost of Equipment at Replacement Cost in a Recession
Labor	$15,000	$15,000	$15,000
Equipment	$30,000	$35,000	$25,000
Profit	$ 5,000	$ 0	$10,000

sition cost of $30,000. Here, it will cost you $45,000 to do the job and you will make a $5,000 profit. Perhaps you should take this job; 10% may not represent an unreasonable profit.

In the second situation, the market replacement value of the inventoried equipment is $35,000. The economy is strong and hence prices are increasing. If you value your inventory at replacement cost, profit is $0. Certainly, you would not take this job.

In the third case, the economy is weak and the market replacement cost for your inventoried equipment is only $25,000. A $10,000, or 20%, profit is attractive, so you take the job.

While there is much to be said for standardization in business decision practices, inventory valuation based on acquisition cost has, in my opinion, been the downfall of many a company. This is especially true in smaller companies which rely on fixed-priced contracts. Indeed, there is an added time burden placed on managers to value periodically inventories based on their replacement cost. The effort to do this often helps the company understand better the cost of carrying more inventory than they really need. It also emphasizes the importance of forecasting demand as accurately as possible.

THE MANAGER'S VIEWPOINT

The ability to compete successfully in the world market depends on how well companies integrate their functional areas of responsibility. One important relationship is the one between production and marketing. Not only should these two groups interact continuously in designing and manufacturing new products, but also they should do the same in anticipation of changes in demand.

Unfortunately, one reason that inventories lag the cycle is because their level is defined after the fact. Inventories are a residual—they are a measure of how well or poorly demand was forecast. If sales are about to slow and no one tells production, what do you think will happen?

It is clear to me from the responses in Table 11.2 that there is a lot of room for improvement in communicating anticipated sales to those who make the products. With better coordination of information, profit will likely increase.

Table 11.2
Managers' Views on Inventory Control

Do your production managers interact regularly with your marketing group in order to set inventory levels?

Type of Company	Always	Sometimes	Never
Manufacturing (40)	1	36	3

ACTION ITEMS

☞ Make sure your forecasts of demand are transmitted to everyone concerned in the company. Remember that inventory levels vary in response to changes in the demand for your product.

☞ Educate your production manager and your production workers to the benefits of understanding how and why the economy is moving.

☞ Create opportunities for dialogue between marketing and production heads so that they both understand what the other is doing and how their actions interrelate.

☞ Formulate a companywide understanding of the linkages between your company, your suppliers, and your customers. Carefully lay out the role of inventories in this inter-connected network.

CHAPTER 12

Capital Budgeting and the Business Cycle

The greatest danger in times of turbulence is not the turbulence; it is to act with yesterday's logic.

Peter Drucker

Capital budgeting is an integral part of business planning. There are three key decisions to make during this process. They relate to investing or not investing in new plant or equipment, how much to invest, and what kind of plant and equipment to buy. Each decision is directly affected by business cycle fluctuations.

WHAT GOES ON IN THE REAL WORLD?

Our production technology is obsolete. Our competitors are building more efficient factories and are using state-of-the art equipment. Without a doubt, they will be making a higher quality product at a lower cost before we even decide what to do. Any ideas?

* * *

If we want to keep our competitive edge, we have to
modernize now. I realize sales are down throughout the
industry, but we need to be forward-looking with our vision of the future. It's only a matter of time before the
Japanese enter the market and we all know what that will
mean. They will come in with a bang. They will have the
most up-to-date technology there is and will get their
products to market faster than we do. The way to stay
ahead is to expand now, update now, and prepare now
for what will be here tomorrow.

These excerpts are not at all unrealistic of what you might
expect to hear in a boardroom or in a senior executives' meeting in
any sized corporation. In fact, the first excerpt is a paraphrase of a
talk given in 1989 by the president of a small tooling and machin-
ing company. The second excerpt is a paraphrase of a speech
made in 1990 by the chairman of the board of a major electronic
components manufacturer at a stockholders' meeting.

The two excerpts contain several similar themes. First, behind
each statement is an implied forecast of what the future has in
store. In the first situation, management realizes they have missed
the boat with regard to keeping their technology up to date. The
rest of the industry thinks market demand will grow. They are anticipating competing for customers on the basis of quality and cost.

In the second situation, management is more farsighted in
their thinking. They are anticipating the need for new technology
in the future and seem to realize that future needs must be decided upon now. They realize their industry will modernize, even
though sales are now down, and that it will become more and
more competitive. This type of anticipatory thinking reflects a perception of the importance of being strategically positioned to capture new customers. Clearly, this chairman understands the importance of being entrepreneurial—perceiving opportunity and
being willing to act upon it.

Whether we are talking about implementing a defensive
(catch-up) strategy or an offensive (take-the-lead) one, information
about the future is critical. There are often situations where you

have to be able to anticipate the direction of industry growth without being overly concerned about short-run cyclical movements around that trend.

Figure 12.1 shows three different anticipated cyclical trends in industry growth. Only the trend in the top diagram reflects prolonged industry growth. Being able to separate a short-run cycle from a long-run trend is critical for effective long-run management. Consider points A1, A2, and A3 in the figure. Different decisions should be made at each of these points, although each corresponds to the same point in the business cycle. In each case, the anticipated long-run trend is more important than the soon to be expected upturn in the business cycle. Capital budgeting involves a long-term commitment.

If there was a situation like the one depicted in the upper diagram of Figure 12.1, and if perceptions/expectations of what competitors are/will be doing are accurate, then I would agree with the decision to make the necessary investments now. Those investments should pay off in the future, especially if the competition is doing the same thing.

CAPITAL BUDGETING DECISIONS

The phrase *capital budgeting* could be misleading to some of you. You would certainly not be the first to be confounded by discipline-specific terminology. First of all, the word *capital* means different things to different people. To those with a background in accounting or finance, the word *capital* refers to operating income. I have used the word *capital* throughout this book in that manner. However, to those trained in economics or to those familiar with policy making, the word *capital* refers to physical plant and equipment, in other words, to tangible, non-labor factors of production. Yes, it is confusing. To complicate matters even more, capital budgeting refers to the budgeting of funds (capital to accountants) to purchase plant and equipment (capital to economists)!

There are three critical decision steps in capital budgeting. These are my own three planning steps; you might come up with five, six, or even a dozen similar decision points by dividing mine

Figure 12.1
Separating Trends from Cycles

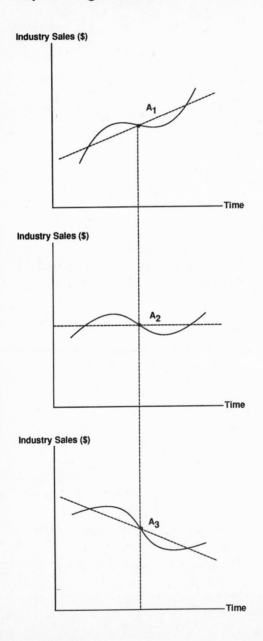

into sub-parts. That would be fine. My concern is to describe the entire process. Your concern as a manager is to implement the capital budgeting process effectively in order to gain a competitive advantage. If your implementation has more finely defined steps than mine, so be it.

I want to use as an example of this process the decision to purchase new equipment (as opposed to expanding plant). My three capital budgeting decisions are:

- invest in new equipment, or not
- how much to invest
- what equipment to buy.

All three of these decisions are directly related to the business cycle, as I alluded to with the diagrams in Figure 12.1.

Invest or Not to Invest

This is the initial decision. An answer can be arrived at in a number of ways, but frequently companies (at least those with whom I have consulted) go about this type of decision planning in one of two ways. One approach relies on what I call MI, referring to managerial intuition. In a purely entrepreneurial manner, instinct may be the sole criterion for investing in new equipment, especially technology-related equipment. It may in fact be a very good criterion, or in some situations the best criterion. A case in point was the way in which a major tobacco products manufacturer in the southeast recently decided to automate their factory. It is my understanding that this decision was made at the top without the aid of any pay-back analysis or financial forecasts. This CEO, I am told, simply believed that the company's competitive survival depended on their ability to reduce costs and control quality through automation . . . and that was that.

From a more objective perspective, financial analyses are frequently used to assist managers to make this go versus no go decision. The basic questions asked—once all of the technical jargon is removed—are two. If we buy the equipment, will the increase in future profit be greater than the cost of the equipment? And if so, will the return be better than what we could earn elsewhere?

I remember quite well *The Wall Street Journal* story in 1988 which described the capital budgeting decisions of many steel companies, both domestic and international. These companies had calculated the cost of automating their nearly 40-year-old technology and the profit potential from these investments, and then they looked at their alternative investments choices. As a result of this simple comparison, many steel companies shut down and invested the proceeds from the sale of their assets elsewhere. In this particular case not only was the automation decision not profitable, the rate of return elsewhere was more attractive than the expected return to be earned from continuing to produce steel in a mature to declining market.

As a less extreme example of the first of these two questions— Will the increase in future profit be greater than the cost of the equipment?—consider the situation illustrated in Figure 12.2. Some new equipment is purchased at time t*. Profit immediately

Figure 12.2
Determining the Profitability of an Investment

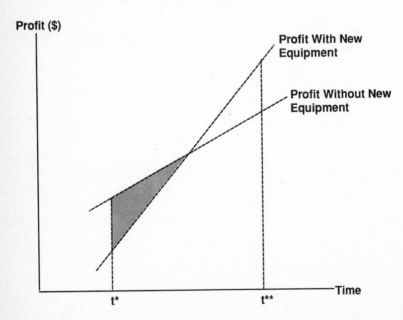

falls, but then it begins to grow at a faster rate than before. Soon, at time t**, profit with the new equipment has increased enough to overcome the cost of the new equipment. Past time t**, the decision to purchase the new equipment looks better and better. As far as the second question—Can we do better elsewhere?—that depends on how long a period of time there is between time t* and time t**. If it will take decades to recover the investment, then it may be that when the investment is recovered the equipment may be obsolete.

I have put some numbers to this invest or not to invest decision. Look at the two cases in Exhibit 12.1. Here, a $400,000 investment is considered in a piece of equipment which has a five-year

Exhibit 12.1
The Invest, Not to Invest Decision

Stream of Profit

$100,000	$110,000	$120,000	$130,000	$140,000
↓	↓	↓	↓	↓
1	2	3	4	5

$400,000
cost

Case 1: $\dfrac{\$100,000}{(1.15)^1} + \dfrac{\$110,000}{(1.15)^2} + \dfrac{\$120,000}{(1.15)^3} + \dfrac{\$130,000}{(1.15)^4} + \dfrac{\$140,000}{(1.15)^5}$

= $392,967 using a 15% discount rate

Case 2: $\dfrac{\$100,000}{(1.08)^1} + \dfrac{\$110,000}{(1.08)^2} + \dfrac{\$120,000}{(1.08)^3} + \dfrac{\$130,000}{(1.08)^4} + \dfrac{\$140,000}{(1.08)^5}$

= $472,995 using an 8% discount rate

life, no maintenance costs, and no scrap value at the end of the fifth year. These last two characteristics are unrealistic, but they simplify the mathematics without distracting from the illustration. This investment in equipment is expected to yield an additional $100,000 in profit after the first year, $110,000 after the second year, and so on in increments of $10,000 for three more years.

Is this a good investment? The answer to that question depends on what discount rate is used when computing the present value of the stream of future profits. Let me elaborate. As the two cases in the Exhibit illustrate, the choice of a higher discount rate, 15%, makes the investment look unprofitable. The present value of the $400,000 investment is $392,967. The choice of a lower discount rate, 8%, would lead you to just the opposite conclusion. The present value of the $400,000 under this condition is $472,995. The fact of the matter is that games are played every day in the business world in order to get the so-called right answer, meaning the answer that you want.

It is not uncommon for the champion of an expansion proposal to, as they say, run the numbers and then arrive at a decision to invest. A more conservative third party (or one with their own agenda) may choose to discount the project at a higher rate and reach an opposite conclusion. Who supervises these manipulations? My advice for those of you who are accountable for the outcome of such investment decisions is to know your discount rate. That is, you should understand what a discount rate represents. It is a measure of the maximum return possible on another investment of comparable risk. Unfortunately, determining the riskiness of an investment is rather subjective. It should be made on the basis of experience with similar investments, as well as with an eye toward the business cycle.

Expectations about business cycle movements are very important in the invest or not to invest decision. First, most major expenditures are financed over time. While the two examples in Exhibit 12.1 show the $400,000 expenditure occurring all at once, this is unrealistic. When considering the cost of financing options, the lower the interest rate changed for financing, the lower the total cost of the equipment. Interest rates move cyclically, and so there is an important timing element to consider when making a long-term investment.

Second, most equipment, especially technologically advanced equipment, is purchased for one of two reasons: to reduce cost or to increase quality. In either case, there must be some implicit expectation about future demand. Demand forms the basis of the cost savings or the sales potential associated with the higher quality product. If the cycle is turning down, then there may be a period before any returns are realized. You may be producing at a lower cost, but total sales are also down. If the cycle is turning up, then the benefits from the investment may materialize sooner.

What the cycle is doing at the present time should not be the critical factor when making a long-run capital budgeting decision. Look again at the top diagram in Figure 12.1. But, what the cycle is doing now should be considered when formulating the financial aspects of the capital budgeting, such as when to incur debt or how to forecast the flow of profit from the investment.

Third, both of the cases in Exhibit 12.1 use calculations where the discount rate remains constant over the five-year period. In reality this is unlikely, although I rarely see a financial analysis of the return from a new piece of equipment which uses a variable discount rate. If the discount rate really does represent the return on alternative investments with comparable risk, then it should change depending on what the business cycle does in the future—five years in the two cases in the Exhibit. In a period of declining interest rates, the choice of a discount rate should reflect the market's expectation of future investment yields.

How Much to Invest

Hand-in-hand with the decision to invest or not to invest is the decision of how much to invest. To use a very simple example, take a small business which decides to invest in computer technology to automate its billing process. Assume the invest or not to invest decision has been made. How much computer technology should then be bought? Should the company purchase exactly what it needs now to meet its current needs, or should future needs be taken into account?

This decision is not independent of the invest or not to invest decision. Often these two decisions are made together. One exception was illustrated in the statement by the chairman of the board that began this chapter. That was a situation where it had been decided already that the equipment investment would be made. What certainly followed was a discussion of how much to invest.

Critical to discussions about how much to invest is an understanding of the concept of diminishing returns. This concept is intuitive, but over and over I see it ignored in capital budgeting exercises. All too frequently I hear the phrase that more is better than less.

Take the case of technical equipment purchased in order to automate a production process. The diagram in Figure 12.3 illustrates the concept of diminishing returns because the returns are increasing less than proportionately to the added technology (the

Figure 12.3
Diminishing Returns to New Technology

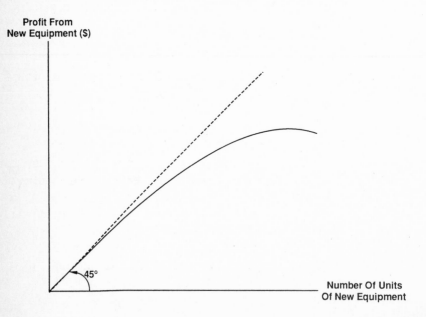

slope of the curve is less than the slope of the 45 degree line). Simply, returns diminish as additional units of the technology are used. This fact does not imply a business would be better off with fewer units, or that it is inefficient to automate fully a production process. It only means one should not think that the benefits from new technology are always proportional to the cost of the technology.

Now we return to the small business considering automating its billing process. It wants to know how powerful of a computer and how fast of a printer it should buy. Let us say that it buys a system which produces a final document in 30 seconds. The cost savings per bill to the company is estimated at $2.00 per bill. If this business later decides to upgrade its equipment so a final document can be produced in only 15 seconds—twice as fast—there is no reason to expect that an additional $1.00 will be saved per bill. There will be diminishing returns to the additional technology. There may be a savings, but if there is, it will not be proportional to the 50% time savings. The reason is that much of the initial savings came from the time saved in going from a manual process to an automated one. Fewer people were involved, hand filing was eliminated, and mistakes were curtailed. Further efficiencies will come more slowly.

What Equipment to Buy

Vendors of equipment are an excellent source of information. The choice of whose equipment to purchase is a difficult one for all of us to make. It took me almost six months to decide which PC to buy for my home office! What most managers are missing is the basic information about what is available and how good it is. Unfortunately, information is costly to acquire. First, there is the time involved in talking with vendors and then separating fact from fiction. Second, there is the issue of serviceability.

There are two important elements in the cost of purchasing new equipment. One is the price, including interest on loans to purchase it. The other is the lost operating time learning how to operate it (there is a difference between making it run and operating it to specification), and how to handle service-related problems. Unfortunately, all operating environments are different.

Rarely will it be the case that the specifications for the equipment's performance are realized exactly in all situations. Perhaps the best rule-of-thumb is to see the equipment in use and talk with other managers about the benefits and costs of dealing with a particular vendor.

There is a cyclical element to consider as well. Equipment vendors, like any other producer of a good or service, have cyclical periods of demand. You may decide to purchase your equipment today, but it may not be available today. Availability depends on the vendors' demand as well as on their production capabilities. This fact should also be included in your decision making process.

THE PSYCHOLOGICAL ASPECTS OF CAPITAL BUDGETING

The title of this section probably sounds odd, and at first blush may seem out of place. I get the same reaction when I speak to groups of executives . . . what are the psychological aspects of capital budgeting?

I frequently observe three types of behavior in the capital budgeting process. First, champions generally overestimate the importance of their ideas. As a result, there is a natural tendency for a champion to exaggerate (often unintentionally) the profit potential, say to purchase a new technology. As the diagram in Figure 12.4 illustrates, it is not uncommon for a champion's profit projection to be higher than those of a more objective observer. This fact is important for you as a manager and perhaps as the individual ultimately responsible for making a financial decision based upon the profit projection. Keep in mind the champion's perspective when evaluating such data as:

- the discount rate used—champions often underestimate the risk associated with their ideas and hence they use a lower than realistic discount rate
- the expected growth rate in profit—champions often use larger estimates either because of their familiarity with the technology or their enthusiasm for the idea

Figure 12.4
The Champion's Perspective on Profit Potential

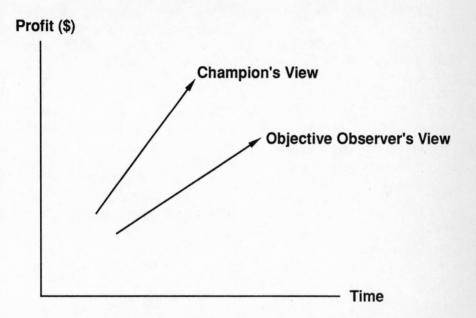

Profit ($)

Champion's View

Objective Observer's View

Time

- the total cost of the new technology—champions who have done their homework and are familiar with the technology will often underestimate the time it takes for others to learn to use the technology.

These psychological aspects of capital budgeting have a cyclical element, too. Frequently, the enthusiasm of a champion is inversely related to the strength of the market. When times are slow, as in a recession, there is often an unconscious pressure on individuals within a business to try to revive things, hence the champion comes forward with the great idea.

There is a natural tendency for most people to underestimate the cost of new plant or equipment. This is true not only for the champion of the idea to purchase the plant or equipment, but it is also true for people in general. In my opinion, this tendency does not reflect any degree of risk aversion. Rather, it is simply human nature. Although I do not have hard data on this point, I would venture to guess that over 95% of capital budgeting analyses use underestimated costs. More than likely the elements that have been underestimated are two: the transitional cost associated with putting the new equipment in place and getting it to work properly, and the human resource cost associated with others learning to operate it. This second aspect of underestimation exists throughout business cycles.

Finally, related to these first two points, is a third tangential issue. People do not like to admit they do not know the answer to a problem. Throughout the capital budgeting process important decisions have to be made. Some of these were discussed earlier in this chapter. At each stage, answers are needed. Are you comfortable telling your boss, "I don't know"? Because of this human tendency, errors may enter into capital budgeting calculations. Such errors include lack of understanding about the nature of the expenditure, especially if it is a new technology; a misperception of the risk of the investment; and most importantly errors in judgment as to whether the investment is needed in the first place. I find that these errors are exaggerated during upswings in the business cycle. During such times people are very busy and frequently pressed with other matters.

The bottom line is that capital budgeting is important. However, you should keep in mind that it is not only an inexact science (if a science at all), but also it is an activity whose accuracy depends on how well cyclical factors are understood and taken into account.

THE MANAGER'S VIEWPOINT

There is an interesting dichotomy in the findings reported in Table 12.1. Top executives, based on information obtained from their chief financial officers, in the manufacturing sector report that they generally do account for (in 32 of 40 cases) the effect of the business cycle in choosing a discount rate. In comparison, only one-third of the top executives in the service sector do so.

Table 12.1
The Discount Rate Used in Capital Budgeting

Based on information gathered from your chief financial officer, does the discount rate used in capital budgeting vary depending on when in the business cycle the analysis is done?

Type of Company	Yes	No
Manufacturing (40)	32	8
Service (15)	5	10

Why is there a difference? In my opinion the manufacturing companies are correctly letting the discount rate be variable. I expect that this may be done less in the service sector due to the shorter life of the purchased equipment.

ACTION ITEMS

☞ Take into account all relevant factors when deciding whether or not to make a long-term capital investment.

☞ Think about using outside consultants in conjunction with in-house analyses of the potential pay-back from a capital investment.

☞ Do not forget that vendors and vendors' customers are excellent resources to use when deciding on new equipment.

CHAPTER 13
Stocks and the Business Cycle

October. This is one of the peculiarly dangerous months to speculate in stocks in. The others are July, January, September, April, November, May, March, June, December, August and February.

Mark Twain

Stock prices fluctuate over time; they generally lead the business cycle. They move in response to investors' demand to own shares in a company. Not all stock prices move together. Some vary more than the market and some vary less. The greater the extent to which managers' salaries are tied to stock options, the greater their incentive to manage in a way which increases stockholder wealth.

Companies raise capital (operating funds) by selling ownership shares in themselves. As you know, capital is essential for operating a business. While there are other ways of raising capital—such as borrowing—many of the larger companies rely on the sale of stock.

Investors purchase stock for two reasons. One is because they anticipate selling it sometime in the future at a higher price. Such a capital gain represents a profit earned on the original investment. The other is because they want to receive dividends.

Managers are well aware of investors' motivations. But, they must also be aware that fluctuating stock prices over the business cycle may cause potential investors to shy away. Fluctuations in the price of a stock or in its dividend payments represent an element of risk. For an investor to accept such risk, there must also be the potential for an above average rate of return.

DO STOCK PRICES MOVE OVER THE BUSINESS CYCLE?

Stock prices lead the business cycle. The diagram in Figure 13.1 clearly illustrates this fact. The indexed price of common stocks has led the business cycle for over 30 years. Historic data (not shown in the figure) would also reveal a similar cyclical pattern throughout this century.

Stock prices fluctuate over the business cycle for several reasons. First and foremost, they fluctuate in direct response to changes in investors' demand to invest in the corporate economy. When demand is weak, stock prices usually fall; when demand is strong, prices usually rise. Why, then, does demand for a particular stock vary?

- Demand is sensitive to expected changes or actual changes in dividend growth. Dividend growth is directly related to the profitability of the company. Because profits are cyclical, it may also be the case that dividend growth is cyclical. While falling stock prices are a normal cyclical phenomenon, few managers would want these fluctuations to be interpreted as being the result of bad management practices. This interpretation might lead stockholders to vote for new management or lead the way for an unfriendly takeover. Therefore, it is not uncommon to see every effort made to maintain dividend stability.

- Interest rate movements also affect investors' tendency to want to buy stocks. Investors have many alternatives. Stocks represent only one of these alternatives. When inter-

Figure 13.1
Stock Price Movements over the Business Cycle

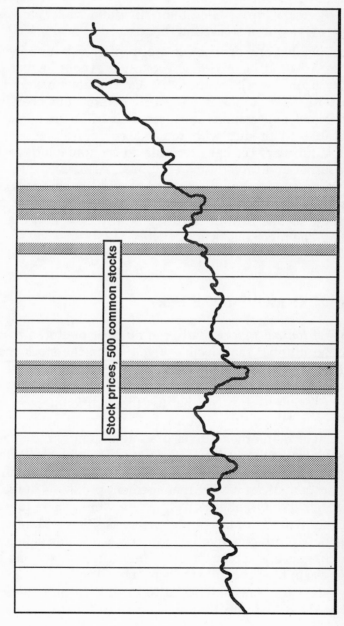

Stock prices, 500 common stocks

1964 65 66 67 68 69 70 71 72 73 74 75 76 77 78 79 80 81 82 83 84 85 86 87 88 89 1990

Source: *Business Conditions Digest.*

est rates increase (as in an expansion) interest rate-sensitive investments become more attractive. For example, when bond yields are greater than dividend yields, investors may move out of stocks into bonds.

- Demand for one or a select group of stocks may increase in expectation of favorable economic events in that company or in the related industry. Expectations have a lot to do with fluctuations in the stock market, but changes in investors' expectations are extremely difficult, if not impossible, to predict with much accuracy (although some consulting services have formulated economic indicators of consumer and investor expectations). Also, as I have noted previously, not all industries move with the business cycle. As well, there may be some unexpected favorable news specific to one firm or industry at any time in a business cycle. The reverse is true as well.

DO ALL STOCKS MOVE TOGETHER?

The Wall Street Journal reports daily the number of stocks that advance and the number that decline. Even when the stock market has a large gain or a large loss, there are a respectable number of stocks that move in the opposite direction.

There are some sound reasons for these differences in stock price movement. When the economy is, say, strong, some companies are stronger than others. Investors might simply move out of the relatively weaker stocks into those with the greater growth potential. Also, even in a cyclical growth industry, there is nothing to prevent a company from having management problems in the face of growing demand. Or, alternatively, there is no reason to expect that a manager would not take an offensive position and introduce a profitable new product when the industry as a whole is faltering.

My comments are applicable over time. On a day-to-day basis there is no reason to expect all stocks to move together, or for that matter, to expect any one individual to be able to pick those that will go up or those that will go down.

The stock market operates, in my opinion and in the opinion of many, in a random walk fashion. This does not mean that all activities are random or that there is not an opportunity for profit. According to Burton Malkiel, author of the popular *A Random Walk Down Wall Street:*

> A random walk is one in which future steps or directions cannot be predicted on the basis of past actions. When the term is applied to the stock market, it means that short-run changes in stock prices cannot be predicted. . . . On Wall Street, the term "random walk" is an obscenity. It is an epithet coined by the academic world and hurled insultingly at the professional soothsayers. Taken to its logical extreme, it means that a blindfolded monkey throwing darts at a newspaper's financial pages could select a portfolio that would do just a well [on a given day] as one carefully selected by experts.

Although the trend in Figure 13.1 shows that the stock market leads the business cycle, some stocks will out perform or under perform others. Of those stocks going up, some will go up more than others, and vice versa.

There is a useful index which describes a stock's systematic variation with the entire market. This index is called a beta coefficient. Based on a theoretical formulation (called the capital asset pricing model) values of beta are always positive.

If a stock has a beta value equal to 1, it means that the stock is of average systematic risk. Of course, a beta coefficient obviously does not account for unexpected events which may occur in the company, the industry, or the economy.

A stock with a beta coefficient of 1.5 will fluctuate, on average, more than the market as a whole. When the market return increases by 1%, the stock's systematic return increases by 1.5%. Such a stock may have downward fluctuations in excess of the market as a whole. Finally, a stock with a beta coefficient of 0.5 is one which has less systematic risk than the market.

Most investment services, such as Standard & Poor's, report a beta coefficient for each stock. Because there is a systematic way to calculate betas, its reported value is generally the same across all investment services.

Investors look at beta coefficients in order to get an idea of the systematic risk embedded in a particular stock. A portfolio of stocks with betas all equal to 1 should, over time, mirror the stock market's overall return. A portfolio with betas greater than 1 should outperform an increasing market and should also fluctuate downward greater than the market as a whole in a downturn. Do keep in mind that betas are calculated on the basis of the historical movements in stock prices relative to the market as a whole.

DO MANAGERS CARE ABOUT STOCK PRICES?

Have you ever known a person who did not care if their invest-ments earned them money? I do not know any such individual.

When a company's stock price goes down, investors—the owners of the company—lose money. Managers, too, may lose es-pecially if their salaries or year-end bonuses are tied to stock op-tions. Collectively, owners have an influence on who is chosen to be on the board of directors and who will be the company presi-dent.

As I explained earlier in the book, there is often a tendency for managers to satisfice. That is, managers often pursue their own professional agenda, at least to some extent, at the expense of com-pany profit. This type of behavior is normal and owners can pro-tect against it only to a degree. One protection, as I have said, is to tie salaries to company performance. Even when this is done, there will still be stock fluctuations. But, these fluctuations will be less influenced by poor management practices than what otherwise might be the case.

The key point to remember is that stock prices fluctuate for economic reasons and for psychological reasons. The latter are not predictable, but nevertheless they still have a pronounced influ-ence.

THE MANAGER'S VIEWPOINT

The responses in Table 13.1 show that company stock prices, even in the same sector, do not move together. As you can see, service company stock prices tend to follow the business cycle fairly closely. However, the top executives of the manufacturing companies report a range of degrees to which their stock prices follow the cycle. There is nothing wrong with these dissimilarities. They simply reflect the nature of the products produced and customers' responsiveness to those products over the business cycle.

Table 13.1
Managers' Views on Stock Price Movements

How does your company's stock price move in relation to the business cycle?

Type of Company	More Than	The Same As	Less Than
Manufacturing (40)	10	18	12
Service (15)	1	12	2

ACTION ITEMS

☞ For those of you in a position to interact with stockholders, emphasize to them the importance of long-term investments versus short-term profit.

☞ Think about line of business diversification as one way to alleviate cyclical fluctuations in your stock prices.

CHAPTER 14

Business Valuations and the Business Cycle

What is a cynic? A man who knows the price of every-
thing, and the value of nothing.

Oscar Wilde

Business valuations are growing in their importance and frequency. The value placed on a closely held company varies over
the business cycle. Several evaluation approaches should be considered before establishing a final estimate of fair market value.

To my knowledge, there are no formal statistics kept on the
number of times each year that businesses are valued. From my
own consulting experience, and from discussions with other
knowledgeable businesspeople, the frequency of valuing companies has increased tremendously over the past several years.

There are at least two reasons for this flurry in business valuation activity. One reason relates to the rapidity with which tax
laws have changed. Valuations are needed to establish the value of

a company before its ownership changes hands—when a business contemplates going from, say, a partnership to a corporation. The other reason relates to the current trend away from diversification. More and more corporations are divesting themselves of tangential product lines. These divestiture efforts, whether outright sales/purchases or partial mergers with other companies, require that the affected line of business be valued.

Valuing public companies is relatively straightforward because the price of the company's stock reflects the market value of the concern. We have all heard of a company being overvalued, meaning that its price-to-earnings ratio is higher than can be justified by its assets; or undervalued, meaning just the opposite. Whatever, the traded price is one reasonable estimate of investors' expectations of the fair market value of a company.

As I discussed in Chapter 13, stock prices lead the business cycle. Therefore, the value investors place on companies moves cyclically. This makes sense. I would be willing to pay a higher price for a company with growing sales than with slack sales. I would be willing to pay a higher price for a company in an industry with growing demand than for one in an industry with waning demand.

CLOSELY HELD BUSINESSES

Not all companies are public. Many, especially smaller ones, are closely held. The ownership of such a company is closely held by one individual, a few individuals, or perhaps a family. There is no publicly traded stock. This form of ownership does not eliminate the need for valuation. Closely held businesses need valuations for tax purposes just like public companies. They too are approached to be bought, and likewise they approach other companies to possibly purchase them.

You, at some time or another, will likely be concerned with valuing a business. Regarding a closely held company, there are two important questions you should ask. What is the fair market value of the business? And, how sensitive is the fair market value estimate to business cycle fluctuations?

FAIR MARKET VALUE

The tax courts have established that the fair market value of a business is the price at which it would change hands in a transaction between a willing buyer and a willing seller. It is useful to have an established definition that is accepted from a legal point of view. However, this definition of fair market value is somewhat problematic. What does the word willing mean?

If no one has offered to buy the closely held business or if no one has attempted to sell it, how do we know what a willing buyer would ask or a willing seller would pay? Does this definition imply that a buy/sell offer must be made before value can be assigned? If only one buy/sell offer is made, how do we know it is fair? What if the two offers are made and they are far apart?

These are reasonable questions. It is easy to see how they are answered for public companies when there are many buyers and sellers bidding on ownership shares every day.

ESTIMATING FAIR MARKET VALUE

There are a number of accepted methods for approximating the fair market value of a closely held business. I will discuss only one in this section. My discussion is not intended to be a guide for how to conduct such a valuation. Business valuations are not back-of-the-envelope calculations. They should not be done solely on the basis of the guidelines offered here. They should be done by experienced economic consultants, accountants, or other credentialed individuals. My goal is only to demonstrate the business cycle-related vagaries associated with business valuations. I want to emphasize the importance of understanding and anticipating business cycles and taking their presence into account when making these decisions.

Ideally, you would like to value a closely held company in terms of comparable public companies. The logic of selecting comparable public companies is straightforward. If the closely held company is very similar to a group of public companies, then its fair market value should be similar (although some adjustments

are generally necessary) to the market-determined value of the
public companies. A fair market value should be independent of
the ownership form of a company.

In practice, finding comparable companies is not always as
easy as it sounds. Most larger companies are diversified. If the
closely held business produces a single good or service, then how
does one compare one line of business to the market's value of
several lines of business? What about new, high-technology products developed to fill a specialized market niche? They may have
no comparables, public or not.

There are standard financial ratios to assist in determining the
degree of comparability of companies. These ratios include, but are
not limited to:

- leverage ratios (e.g., total debt to total assets)
- liquidity ratios (e.g., current assets to current liabilities)
- profit ratios (e.g., income to sales).

By comparing the ratios between public and closely held companies you can determine *approximately* how comparable the businesses are.

Finding comparable companies is critical to establishing the
fair market value of a business. The use of these financial ratios is
widely accepted, but I still will offer you several words of caution.
My words of caution are from a managerial perspective rather
than from a legal or accounting perspective.

Just because two companies compare well in terms of standard financial ratios does not necessarily mean they are comparable in value. Both companies may be broadly classified in the same
industry, which seems to me to be a prerequisite condition. But,
the diversified public companies' ratios may reflect the financial
activities of many lines of business whereas the closely held company may have only one line of business. There is no way to tell
from published company-level financial statements which line of
business, if any, is best reflected by the aggregate data. Therefore,
you might be using financial ratios averaged over several lines of
business to compare to a single line of business company. This

would not be so bad if all the lines of business follow the business cycle in the same way. Who knows if that is the case?

Putting this issue of diversification aside—and there is not much that can be done about it anyway—there still are at least two other problems which must be addressed when selecting a set of comparable companies. Public companies in the same industry not only have different levels of managerial expertise, but also may mirror the market differently.

Regarding managerial expertise, this important aspect of a company is only partially captured in the company's stock price. If the economy is booming and sales are rapidly growing, then the stock market will give less of a premium to such managerial expertise than when the economy is falling. When the economy is near a recession, the market will often give a premium to such well-managed companies based on the expectation that these companies will outlive the recession and rebound faster when the economy turns up.

Ignoring managerial issues for the moment, we know some company stock prices fluctuate more that others over the business cycle. Two companies in the same industry with similar financial ratios might have very different betas, say 0.8 versus 1.2. Clearly these two companies will have different stock prices and earnings at different points of the business cycle.

Although these cycle-related issues are somewhat abstract, discussing them does illustrate that business valuation is less than an exact science. It is, in fact, an exercise subject to business cycle error. Unfortunately, when there is a need to value a business a best estimate must be made.

Data on comparable companies are often used as follows. You might calculate the earnings per share of the closely held company (E/S) and then multiply it by the average price earning ratio (P/E) of the group of comparable businesses. The product approximates the price per share (P/S) of the closely held company:

$$E/S \times P/E = P/S.$$

Some call this approach the capitalized earnings approach to fair market value. One way to use this approach, and to correct for cyclical factors present in the analysis, is to use an earnings per share and price earnings ratio averaged over some reasonable period of time. An example of the capitalized earnings approach to establishing fair market value is detailed in Exhibit 14.1.

VIEWING A BUSINESS AS AN ANNUITY

An alternative business valuation approach which I favor is not based on the use of comparable company data. Rather, I like to view the purchase of a closely held business as an investment which is expected to yield a return over a period of time, say 20 or 30 years. In reality, why would someone want to buy a company if not for its investment potential? Viewed this way, an alternative approach to calculating the fair market value of a business is to calculate the expected present value of the cash flow (and I prefer

Exhibit 14.1
The Capitalized Earnings Approach to Valuing a Closely Held Company

An illustrative outline of the calculations for this type of analysis:

The earnings per share (E/S) of the closely held company to be valued is $2.
$$E/S = \$2.$$

The price earnings ratio (P/E) of a group of comparable companies is 15.
$$P/E = 15.$$

The price per share of the closely held company to be valued is 30.
$$P/S = E/S \times P/E = \$2 \times 15 = \$30.$$

If there are 100,000 shares of closely held stock (S = 100,000), then the fair market value of this company is approximated as $3,000,000.
$$P = \$30 \times S = \$30 \times 100,000 = \$3,000,000.$$

cash flow to net income) stream generated by the business. Some call this a discounted cash flow approach to business valuation.

This approach implies that a willing buyer would value a business in terms of the present value of the cash flow that it could produce over time. Specific to this calculation are three key pieces of information:

- the cash flow of the business, probably averaged over several previous years
- an expected annual growth rate in cash flow over future years
- a discount rate.

The cash flow of the business being valued is embedded in every company's financial statement. What is difficult to determine is what growth rate to use in this calculation. You might decide to use the growth rate over the previous few years. That may or may not be accurate depending on what the business cycle was doing. The growth rate in cash flow would be directly related to the growth rate of sales, and the growth rate of sales depends on the health of the economy. Also, the growth rate that will apply in the future depends on someone's expectations of how well the business will do and what the state of the economy will be. The seller of the business will, for obvious reasons, estimate this growth rate higher than would a potential purchaser. But there will be variations among purchasers, too. Unfortunately, there is no formula to use in determining which future growth rate is the most accurate. That is why different people value businesses differently.

The choice of a discount rate is less bothersome, but not without its own problems. Keep in mind that interest rates vary over the business cycle. Today's interest rate or an average of previous interest rates is not, in my opinion, a good choice. Perhaps the best choice, and one which incorporates investors' expectations of future events, is a long-term rate on bonds which reflects the type of risk associated with the business. If the business is risk free (hypothetically speaking) then the current rate offered on a 30-year government bond may be applicable. Or, you might use the corporate bond rate which corresponds to companies with similar risk. Or, you might use the rate which corresponds to the rate a financial institution has recently charged the business being valued for loans.

In my opinion this annuity-like approach to business valuation avoids some of the cyclical problems inherent in the more traditional approaches. An example of my annuity approach is detailed in Exhibit 14.2.

THE MANAGER'S VIEWPOINT

Top executives in both the manufacturing and service sectors share my belief that the incidence of business valuations has increased sharply over the past five years. See Table 14.1. Upon asking them about their impression of the reasons for this trend, they responded almost unanimously that they were due to changes in the tax laws.

Exhibit 14.2
The Present Value of Cash Flow Approach to Valuing a Closely Held Company

An illustrative outline of the calculations for this type of analysis:

The average cash flow of the closely held company to be valued, calculated from three years of previous data, is $100,000.

The average annual rate of growth in cash flow over these past three years is 11.5%.

The present value of cash flow over the next 30 years, assuming an 11.5% growth and a discount rate of 9%, is $4,346,147.

$$PV = \sum_{t=1}^{30} \$100{,}000 \times (1.115)^t / (1.09)^t = \$4{,}346{,}147.$$

Table 14.1
Managers' Views about the Incidence of
Business Valuations

What is your perception about the frequency of business valuations in your industry? Have they increased/stayed the same/decreased over the past five years?

Type of Company	Increased	Stayed the Same	Decreased
Manufacturing (40)	31	9	0
Service (15)	9	6	0

ACTION ITEMS

☞ Learn about the enterprise being valued. Do not let your managerial opinions be formulated solely on the basis of someone else's numbers. Keep your instinct keen.

☞ Obtain several expert opinions when valuing a closely held business. Use several valuation techniques, too.

☞ Use leading economic indicators to help you instinctively value the concern in question.

CHAPTER 15

When to Ignore the Business Cycle

Every man takes the limits of his own field of vision for the limits of the world.

Arthur Schopenhauer

In 1987 the editorial staff of the *Harvard Business Review* asked its readers: "Do you think there is a competitiveness problem?" The answer from nearly 4,000 readers was an overwhelming "yes."

Over 92 percent of these readers believed then, and probably still do now, that U.S. competitiveness is deteriorating. Because of this deterioration, our standard of living is threatened, as is the economic position of our country in the world market.

How did this predicament develop? America used to be the prominent economic power in the world. The popular press has identified three culprits: workers, managers, and the federal government. Not surprisingly, their recommended solutions are equally as well focused: work harder, manage better, and pass more protective policies!

Academics have been more systematic in their study of the deterioration of America's competitiveness. They have identified, through numerous statistical studies, a number of problem areas:

- the adverse impact of labor unions on worker productivity
- the energy crisis in the early 1970s which rendered many production facilities uneconomical to operate
- too many government regulations—compliance with these regulations diverted productive energies away from competitive activities
- declining saving rates which led to an increase in interest rates and thus an increase in the cost of building new plants and buying new equipment
- a relative decline in America's educational system and its failure to produce the types of industrial leaders that many think we need
- a growing prevalence of what I call managerial myopia.

This is not the place to debate the relative merits of any one of these suggested sources. In this chapter I want to concentrate on only the last issue, managerial myopia. I particularly want to emphasize that there are times when you, in your capacity as both a manager as well as a leader, need to ignore the business cycle and make long-term commitments based on instinct rather than on financial formulae.

Before doing so, I must warn you that I am not going to cover completely the issue of managerial myopia. What follows is not a comprehensive list of all areas where managers' shortsightedness has contributed to America's woes.

My intent here is more focused. First, I want to create some dissonance. I want you to think about all of the business cycle planning guidelines raised in the previous chapters in comparison to the prescriptions offered here. Second, I want to charge you to think beyond the confines of your current environment and to kindle in you a spark of responsibility for the future of America.

You may recall from the Preface that this book "is directed toward owners, managers, and advisors of growing businesses who wish to take a more sophisticated approach to business planning and decision making." Throughout the book I have offered words of caution about the importance of timing your decisions to take into account business cycle fluctuations. I was serious when making these recommendations. But there are also important decisions which require a vision far beyond the next business cycle or two. Many of these decisions defy the cost-benefit ratios or rate of return models used by finance and accounting consultants.

WHY ARE AMERICAN MANAGERS SHORTSIGHTED?

For the most part, American managers are very shortsighted in their decision making. Because of that, America is in its current competitive dilemma.

> What accounts for the short-term bias in American industry? Is it that U.S. firms tend to . . . focus on the short term because they are somehow incapable of looking as far ahead as their overseas rivals? Or are they forced by external circumstances—the macroeconomic environment or the cultural bias of American society—to focus on the short term, even though they realize that it is not in their best interest to do so? Or might it be that a short-term focus is in the best interest of individual firms, but not of the U.S. economy as a whole?
> MIT Commission on Industrial Productivity

Managers act in their own self-interest subject to the constraints of their position. The important objectives of every manager I know are either job mobility and/or job security. This is true for managers on every step of the public sector or private sector corporate ladder.

What are the prerequisites for promotion? Promotion is often based on your ability to demonstrate success in managing projects or in making key decisions. The implication of this reward structure is clear. If you want to succeed, you must have something to show from your past efforts.

It seems to me that what probably concerns many fledgling managers are ways to put together a portfolio of successfully completed projects. The shorter the time frame of each project, the more projects there will be in a particular period of time. The less risky the projects, the more of them that will be successful.

Where did such a count-them-up incentive structure originate? Senior executives face similar pressures, and these pressures work their way through an organization. Senior executives are obligated to maximize the short-term profit of the company so they will not be penalized by investors through stock price fluctuations. Company owners—stockholders—are preoccupied with dividends and earnings; it is no surprise that senior executives are similarly preoccupied. It is also no surprise that in March 1990, *Business Week* editorialized in its cover story that non-profit corporations are some of the most efficiently run organizations in America.

We all know, at least intuitively, that research and development (R&D) drives the innovation process. Without it, most companies would not have the innovative new products needed in order to compete year after year in growing world markets. But why is it that when quarterly profit levels fall, many American companies first cut back on their R&D expenditures in order to maintain their short-term profit margins? Might their reactions be related to the fact that many senior executives are more interested in jumping from company to company in order to increase their salary and position rather than in making the needed long-term commitment to growth (and staying around long enough to see it occur)?

WHAT NEEDS TO CHANGE?

I am not suggesting that you ignore the impact business cycle fluctuations can have on your company's performance. On the contrary, that is precisely what this book is all about. I am also not suggesting that you, regardless of your position, enslave yourself to one particular job or ignore promotion possibilities or new job opportunities.

As an economist by training, I teach my students the economic efficiencies gained when individuals pursue their own self-interest. Self-interest on the part of both consumers and producers leads to market efficiency. It is rational for stockholders to want to earn as high a return on their investments as possible. It is rational for managers to seek promotions and to respond to the incentive structures within their company. And, it is rational for senior executives to protect their careers by appeasing their constituents.

However, we do have a predicament:

- owners of companies want to see short-run financial results
- managers see it is in their best interest to make decisions which will deliver what the owners want
- competitive survival in growing world markets requires farsightedness, long-term commitments to R&D and quality, and risk taking.

I do not think an investor or a manager will change his behavior just because I say it is important for our economy for them to do so. I also do not think the government has a significant role to play in initiating such change, although there are areas where the government can assist in the innovation process. I do think the impetus for change can come from the educational system in our country. What is needed is a new mind-set; one developed through educational-related initiatives.

We must rethink the way business students and MBAs are taught. I know of no business curriculum offering a course called Commitment 600. Who would teach it? What faculty member would give up their research time to prepare it? Remember, research output is the primary way faculty are evaluated for promotion, tenure, and salary adjustments. And what curriculum committee would pass such a course? Who could agree on the course syllabus?

Such a course probably will never come to pass. That is probably for the best because commitment is really not an academic subject. Commitment is a mind-set, one which was present in American managers through the history of its industrial development, but one which has become lost in the pages of leveraged buyouts, merger agreements, and golden parachutes. By commitment I mean more than dedication, although that is important too. I associate commitment with entrepreneurship.

To me, an entrepreneur is an individual who perceives opportunity and has the courage and conviction to act upon that perception. In today's market, stockholders reward successful actions and penalize failures; managers are rewarded for countable successes not for championing ideas. This is all very rational behavior by short-term profit maximizing agents. But it might just change, and if it does, it will have to change from within. It will change from the bottom up—initiated by those fledgling managers who have the courage to follow through on their educationally based convictions and perceptions, and reinforced by those senior executives who have the self-confidence to stand in front of stockholders and tell them where the company is now and where it can be in the future (and what will happen along the way).

Cycles are cycles. They come and go. I hope entrepreneurship is here forever. And if it is, I would venture a guess that the companies who foster it will also be around.

The Manager's Viewpoint in Detail

In an effort to provide additional dimensions of realism and practicality to the guidelines outlined in this book, I surveyed presidents/CEOs of U.S. companies. I wanted their opinions on the chapter topics covered. These individuals' companies were selected randomly from the largest manufacturing companies, the largest service companies, and the newest high-technology companies in America. My sources were *Fortune, Business Week,* and *High Technology Business.*

The survey interviewing continued until I had received (in 1990) complete information from:

40 manufacturing companies
15 service companies
15 high-tech companies.

I will not try to convince anyone that the information summarized in each chapter perfectly reflects the opinions and actions of corporate America, but my consulting and research experiences with these and similar companies gives me confidence that their collected behavior is fairly representative of the real world.

APPENDIX A.2
Factors Affecting Aggregate Supply and Demand

Fiscal policy and monetary policy are the two primary tools the government uses to influence the direction of the economy. Simply, fiscal policy influences aggregate demand directly and monetary policy affects it indirectly. Fiscal policy works through the C, I, and G components of GNP to affect aggregate demand, and monetary policy affects interest rates which in turn affect C and I. I am ignoring exports and imports and international currency markets in this explanation, but they are also important.

Think of the economy as three markets working together. These three markets are the output market, the labor market, and the money market. As with any market, there is a product and a price. The product in the output market is real GNP and the price is an average price index. In the labor market these two variables are the aggregate level of employment and an average wage level. And in the money market they are the quantity of money and the interest rate (although there are numerous interest rates prevailing in the economy, they all tend to move together).

Fiscal policy used to, say, expand the economy generally takes two forms: a reduction in personal and/or corporate tax rates and an increase in government purchases. Treating these individually, although they can be implemented together, illustrates the market interactions mentioned throughout the book. A decrease in taxes increases consumption (C) and investment (I). As a result, aggregate demand increases and there is upward pressure on prices. To produce this additional aggregate output, the demand for labor also increases (unemployment falls) putting upward pressure on wages. An increase in government purchases produces the same result but it works through the G component of GNP.

Of course, ours is a dynamic economy so GNP and prices do not simply go up and down. Rather, the rate of growth in these and other key economic variables increases and decreases.

Monetary policy is conducted by the Federal Reserve System (Fed). An increase in the supply of money (brought about most often by a purchase of government securities by the Fed) will increase the supply of money in the money market. As a result, the price of money, the interest rate, will fall. In response to lower interest rates, consumption (C) and investment (I) will increase and so does aggregate demand. As with fiscal policy, the demand for labor will also increase.

Both of the illustrations here are expansionary, meaning that the desired result was an increase in real GNP. With this increase comes higher prices and wages, lower levels of unemployment, and lower interest rates.

Albeit simple, this explanation is a fairly accurate representation of how the economy works and how markets interrelate.

APPENDIX A.3
Managerial Forecasting Techniques

You must decide on the tradeoffs you are willing to make when selecting among forecasting techniques. Generally, accuracy comes at the expense of cost and ease of use. The more simple techniques, that is, those that can be done easily in-house, are generally less accurate. Most managers, limited by resources and time, will choose a middle ground.

Forecasting techniques fall into three broad categories: judgment or qualitative techniques, time series analysis, and causal models.

Judgment techniques are used when data are scarce and/or when only a rough-and-ready forecast of sales (or some other performance variable) is needed. This type of analysis is basically an opinion-based extrapolation of previous sales activity: "I think we can expect the same average annual rate of growth over the next ten years as we had last year." Sometimes corporate officers will employ a Delphi technique. This involves a series of successive estimates by knowledgeable individuals about the future potential for sales. But still, personal judgments dominate.

Time series analysis is more complex. It relies on various statistical methods to separate out patterns of movement from historical data. Because historical data are used here, time series analysis is a form of extrapolation. However, time series techniques have the important capability to allow the forecaster to decompose historical patterns into seasonal, cyclical, and time trends. This thus permits a more accurate forecast as long as you believe that previous patterns will continue into the future.

Causal models are the most sophisticated. You would first identify quantitatively those factors which are correlated with the growth of sales. Your marketing staff may have the statistical expertise to do this, or you may rely on consultants. Whichever, once the causal factors are identified, you simply need to monitor changes in them so as to be able to predict the magnitude of the changes in sales that will follow. For example, one causal factor which influences housing sales is the long-term rate of interest. Another more local variable in such a causal model would be the age profile of the locality.

The applicability of any particular technique is sensitive to the business cycle. You must be certain about the future state of the economy before you rely financially on your forecasts. For example, I would be careful about forecasting future sales based on past sales if the past five years, say, have been boom years and every indicator predicts a downturn in the near future. Also, some forecasting techniques are more applicable than others over the life of a new product. For example, during the product development stage, judgment methods are, I think, the most appropriate. This seems obvious because no historical data are available. During the initial growth stage, I often recommend not using a forecasting technique. Rather, I recommend paying close attention to the opinions of sales and marketing personnel in order to gain firsthand information about the strength of the market. Should you feel their opinions are not accurate, then perhaps you have a personnel problem rather than a forecasting problem. Finally, in a steady state stage of growth for the company, time series analysis and causal models are the most appropriate, in my view.

Glossary of Terms

AGGREGATE ECONOMIC PROFIT: Aggregate economic profit is calculated as gross national product less indirect business taxes, depreciation, the total wage bill, and interest paid by businesses. This is a leading economic indicator.

BETA COEFFICIENT: A beta coefficient is a number (based on theoretical calculations) which reflects how a particular stock has historically moved with the stock market as a whole. If a particular stock has a beta greater (less) than 1 then that stock is considered to have more systematic risk (less systematic risk) than the average of all stocks in the market.

BOOM: A prolonged period of economic growth in the expansion phase of a business cycle is a boom. It is that period leading to a business cycle peak.

BUSINESS CYCLE: A business cycle is a sequence of expansions and contractions in various economic processes which show up as major fluctuations in aggregate economic activity—that is, in comprehensive measures of production, employment, income, and trade.

175

BUSINESS PROFIT: Business profit is calculated as sales revenue less returns and allowances, indirect business taxes, depreciation, payroll, interest expenses, and cost of goods sold.

CAPITAL BUDGETING: The process of capital budgeting refers to the budgeting of funds to purchase new plant and equipment. This process involves a number of decisions ranging from the initial decision to invest or not, to what equipment to buy.

CAPITALIZED EARNINGS APPROACH TO FAIR MARKET VALUE: Using this approach, the fair market value of a closely held company is approximated by using the earnings per share of the closely held company to be valued and the average price earnings ratio of a group of comparable companies.

CIRCULAR FLOW: An illustration of the movement between consumers and producers of both final goods and services and factors used in the production process.

COINCIDENT ECONOMIC INDICATORS: Coincident indicators move with the business cycle. The government publishes a composite series of four such indicators. This series is useful for verifying turning points in business cycles.

CONSUMER PRICE INDEX: The consumer price index (CPI) is an average price level for a market basket of final goods and services. This market basket is intended to represent the buying habits of an estimated 80 percent of the U.S. population. Approximately 400 items are in this market basket, including food, apparel, transportation, health services, housing, and recreation. Prices of these goods and services are obtained by regularly surveying 85 different geographical areas within the United States.

CONSUMPTION: Consumption by households is one of the four major components of GNP. It includes all expenditures on domestic goods and services except residential housing. These expenditures account for about 65 percent of total expenditures in the United States in a given year.

CONTRACTION: The contraction phase of the business cycle is that period when economic activity is declining. There are two stages of a contraction, the initial stage or slowdown and the secondary stage or recession.

COST-PLUS PRICING: This is a pricing strategy whereby a company sets its final price at a level which corresponds to its production costs plus a profit factor.

DEBT: Issuing debt or bonds is one way corporations acquire operating funds. A bond is a corporate IOU telling the holder the rate of interest the issuing company will pay on its borrowed funds and the date when the principal will be repaid.

DISCOUNTED CASH FLOW APPROACH TO BUSINESS VALUATION: This approach to valuing a closely held company is based on calculating the present value of the company's expected future stream of cash flow.

ECONOMIC INDICATOR: An economic indicator is a series of data which corresponds to movements in economic activity. Changes in economic indicators signal changes in various aspects of economic activity.

ELASTICITY OF DEMAND: This is a measure of how responsive consumers are to a change in producers' prices.

EQUITY: Issuing stock or equity is one way which corporations acquire operating funds. Stock represents ownership in a corporation. As such, the owner of stock is entitled to share in the profit of the company, usually in the form of dividend payments.

EXPANSION: The expansion phase of the business cycle is that period when economic activity is increasing. There are two stages of an expansion, the recovery stage when economic activity initially begins to increase and the boom stage when economic activity is growing vigorously.

FISCAL POLICY: Fiscal policy refers to any government policy which directly affects aggregate demand. The most common ways the government attempts to stabilize the economy are through changes in taxes or changes in government purchases.

GROSS NATIONAL PRODUCT: GNP represents the current dollar value of all final goods and services sold in the U.S. economy in a given year. GNP equals the sum of the purchases made by the four main components of the economy. These are consumption (C), investment (I), government purchases (G), and net exports (NX). The accounting of GNP is often summarized as GNP = C + I + G + NX.

GNP DEFLATOR: The GNP deflator, or implicit price deflator for GNP, is an average price level of the economy's current output including consumption, investment, government purchases, and net exports. This index reflects average price movements in the relevant goods and services in each of the four component categories of GNP. Most economists and policy makers view the GNP deflator as the most relevant economywide index of inflation.

GOVERNMENT PURCHASES: Government purchases is one of the four major components of GNP. It represents expenditures on military equipment; the employment of the armed forces and other government workers; and the provision of roads, bridges, and other public goods and services—the nation's infrastructure. There is an important distinction between government purchases and government expenditures. Government expenditures exceed government purchases by the amount spent on both benefit payments (e.g., Social Security) and the interest expense on government debt.

INFLATION: Inflation refers to a period of continuous increase in average prices. A corresponding period of continuous decrease in prices is a deflation.

INTEREST RATE: An interest rate is the price of borrowing money; therefore, its level influences the quantity of borrowing in the economy. Higher interest rates reduce borrowing and thus dampen economic growth. Interest rates generally increase in an expansion and decrease in a contraction.

INVESTMENT: Investment is one of the four major components of GNP. Investment expenditures include fixed business investment (the purchase of plant and equipment by firms), residential construction, and changes in inventories. These expenditures account for about 16% of GNP in a given year.

LAGGING ECONOMIC INDICATORS: The government's composite index of seven lagging indicators lags swings in the business cycle. This index turns up after a trough and it turns down after a peak.

LEADING ECONOMIC INDICATORS: Leading economic indicators foretell cyclical swings in the economy. The government publishes a composite index of 11 such indicators. Historically, leading indicators have predicted an upturn in the business cycle fewer months ahead of time than they have predicted a downturn.

MONETARY POLICY: Monetary policy refers to government policy which affects economy activity through changes in the money supply. The transmission of the effects of a monetary policy is through the resulting changes in interest rates.

NATIONAL BUREAU OF ECONOMIC RESEARCH: NBER is a private organization which conducts research on business cycles, among other topics. Its researchers have the responsibility for dating the peaks and troughs of U.S. business cycles and for preparing economic indicators of the economy.

NET EXPORTS: Net exports are one of the four major components of GNP. They include the balance of trade (the export minus the import of goods) and the balance of services (the export minus the import of services). Net exports were negative in the late 1980s meaning that imports were greater than exports.

OUTPUT PER WORKER: Q/L is perhaps the most common, but not necessarily the most accurate, way to measure labor productivity. This index is calculated by dividing a measure of output by either the number of workers used to produce the products or the total amount of time used for production.

PRICE DISCRIMINATION: This is a pricing strategy whereby producers charge different prices to different segments of consumers, such as children and senior citizens.

PRODUCT LIFE CYCLE: In general, the sales-related life of a product is cyclical. The product life cycle is a graphical illustration of this fact. It is divided into four parts. When a new product is introduced into the market, industry sales first increase slowly (Introduction), then more rapidly (Growth), and eventually begin to level off (Maturity), and then decline (Decline).

PRODUCTION PROCESS LIFE CYCLE: The production process life cycle refers to the various production changes made by companies over the life of a product. As such, it is closely tied to the product life cycle.

RECESSION: A recession is a prolonged period of economic decline leading to a business cycle trough.

RECOVERY: An economic recovery refers to the initial period of growth following a business cycle trough.

RETAIL LIFE CYCLE: This term refers to the periodic introduction of retailing innovations. As with any new product, these innovations will grow and declin in use over time.

SLOWDOWN: An economic slowdown refers to the initial stage of a contraction in the business cycle. It is the initial period of decline following a peak.

SATISFICING: This term refers to the fact that most managers pursue their own self-interest. As such, they operate at a level less than the one that maximizes owners' wealth. Rather, they seek to provide only a minimum acceptable level of company performance. Managers' remaining efforts go to maximizing their own self-interest.

TOTAL FACTOR PRODUCTIVITY: TFP is a measure of productivity. It is calculated by dividing the level of output produced by the amount of all factors used in production.

UNEMPLOYMENT: The labor force is defined as all persons 16 years or older who are actively seeking employment or who are currently employed. The unemployment rate is the portion of the labor force unemployed.

Index

About the Author

ALBERT N. LINK is both a noted academician and consultant.

Having received his Ph.D. in economics from Tulane University (1976), Professor Link is now Director of the MBA Program at the University of North Carolina at Greensboro. He has previously been Head of the Department of Economics, Director of the Industrial Technology Program, and Director of the Computer Technology Education Program at the University. In his capacity as Professor of Economics, he has written over 50 scholarly articles which have appeared in the most prestigious economics, business, engineering and policy journals. He has also lectured on a variety of topics throughout the United States as well as in Austria, Germany, France, Korea, and England. In 1989, he was a U.S. Delegate to the Republic of Korea participating in the First Korea-United States Conference on Science and Technology Policy.

Professor Link is the author of 12 books on topics ranging from entrepreneurship to corporate strategy. He is the co-author of *The Complete Executive's Encyclopedia of Accounting, Finance, Investing, Banking & Economics* (Probus Publishing Company).

Also, Professor Link regularly consults for major U.S. and international corporations and governmental agencies on a variety of issues ranging from business valuations, to productivity, to technology management.